CAMBRIDGE LIBRARY COLLECTION

Books of enduring scholarly value

Travel and Exploration

The history of travel writing dates back to the Bible, Caesar, the Vikings and the Crusaders, and its many themes include war, trade, science and recreation. Explorers from Columbus to Cook charted lands not previously visited by Western travellers, and were followed by merchants, missionaries, and colonists, who wrote accounts of their experiences. The development of steam power in the nineteenth century provided opportunities for increasing numbers of 'ordinary' people to travel further, more economically, and more safely, and resulted in great enthusiasm for travel writing among the reading public. Works included in this series range from first-hand descriptions of previously unrecorded places, to literary accounts of the strange habits of foreigners, to examples of the burgeoning numbers of guidebooks produced to satisfy the needs of a new kind of traveller - the tourist.

Franklin's Footsteps

Clement Robert Markham (1830–1916) was a geographer who took part in one of the many Arctic expeditions launched to search for missing explorer John Franklin (1786–1847). This account, published in 1853, was written in response to criticism of the expedition. They had found some evidence of Franklin's route – he had set off in May 1845 to find the North-West Passage – but returned to Britain without any of the survivors. Markham gives a brief history of Arctic exploration, but the majority of the book recounts the expedition's efforts to find Franklin. The crew endured a harsh winter and sailed in iceberg-laden waters along the coast of Greenland, looking for clues of Franklin's whereabouts. They also spent some time exploring the Parry Islands (the present-day Queen Elizabeth Islands). Markham's account of the rescue mission provides insight into the little-known and often dangerous world of Arctic explorers.

Cambridge University Press has long been a pioneer in the reissuing of out-of-print titles from its own backlist, producing digital reprints of books that are still sought after by scholars and students but could not be reprinted economically using traditional technology. The Cambridge Library Collection extends this activity to a wider range of books which are still of importance to researchers and professionals, either for the source material they contain, or as landmarks in the history of their academic discipline.

Drawing from the world-renowned collections in the Cambridge University Library and other partner libraries, and guided by the advice of experts in each subject area, Cambridge University Press is using state-of-the-art scanning machines in its own Printing House to capture the content of each book selected for inclusion. The files are processed to give a consistently clear, crisp image, and the books finished to the high quality standard for which the Press is recognised around the world. The latest print-on-demand technology ensures that the books will remain available indefinitely, and that orders for single or multiple copies can quickly be supplied.

The Cambridge Library Collection brings back to life books of enduring scholarly value (including out-of-copyright works originally issued by other publishers) across a wide range of disciplines in the humanities and social sciences and in science and technology.

Franklin's Footsteps

*A Sketch of Greenland,
Along the Shores of which
His Expedition Passed,
and of the Parry Isles,
where the Last Traces
of It Were Found*

CLEMENTS R. MARKHAM

CAMBRIDGE
UNIVERSITY PRESS

CAMBRIDGE UNIVERSITY PRESS

Cambridge, New York, Melbourne, Madrid, Cape Town,
Singapore, São Paolo, Delhi, Mexico City

Published in the United States of America by Cambridge University Press, New York

www.cambridge.org
Information on this title: www.cambridge.org/9781108048385

© in this compilation Cambridge University Press 2012

This edition first published 1853
This digitally printed version 2012

ISBN 978-1-108-04838-5 Paperback

FRANKLIN'S FOOTSTEPS

A SKETCH OF GREENLAND,

ALONG THE

SHORES OF WHICH HIS EXPEDITION PASSED,

AND OF

The Parry Isles,

WHERE THE LAST TRACES OF IT WERE FOUND.

BY

CLEMENT ROBERT MARKHAM,

LATE OF H.M.S. ASSISTANCE.

LONDON:

CHAPMAN AND HALL, 193, PICCADILLY.

1853.

PRINTED BY
JOHN EDWARD TAYLOR, LITTLE QUEEN STREET,
LINCOLN'S INN FIELDS.

PREFACE.

THE object of the following pages is to lead the
reader in Sir John Franklin's footsteps to the
verge of the yet unknown tracts of country in the
Arctic Regions; to attain this, I have endeavoured
to give a slight sketch of the countries along the
shores of which he is supposed to have passed, and
I have tracked him and his gallant companions
until both are lost to our mental view. In the in-
troductory chapter I have shown how and when
Greenland was discovered by the Normans, and
have recorded the valorous deeds and daring adventures of that hardy race in those northern lands.
I have also enumerated the various Expeditions to
Baffin's Bay and Greenland, of the navigators of
the age of Elizabeth; and shortly alluded to the
enterprising exertions of the Danish and Moravian
Missionaries. The remainder of the first part of this

little work deals more at large with the voyages of those embarked in the whale-fishery; and comprises a brief account of the modern Expeditions in search of a North-west Passage by way of Baffin's Bay and Lancaster Sound, which have unfortunately concluded in the disappearance of Sir John Franklin's vessels. What follows is a narrative of the Expedition under the command of Captain Austin, in 1850–51, in search of the missing ships and their ill-fated crews; and in this Expedition I was one of the humblest as well as one of the youngest labourers. Thus I have endeavoured to furnish the reader, at one view, and in a condensed form, with a connected history of what has been done by way of discovery in the ice-bound regions of the north from the earliest periods to the present time, as well as with a detailed narrative of the means that have been employed towards rescuing those of our brave countrymen who have been so long lost in those trackless and inhospitable regions.

C. R. M.

EDITOR'S PREFACE.

SINCE the following pages were in the printer's hands there have appeared no less than three distinct works upon the same subject: Lieutenant Osborn, Dr. Sutherland, and Captain Mangles, have each separately recorded their experiences in the Arctic Regions, and expressed their opinions as to the fate of Sir John Franklin and his gallant companions. The author of 'Franklin's Footsteps' had, ever since his return with Captain Austin's Expedition, determined on submitting the result of his own observations and researches—slight and imperfect as some may deem them—to the public, feeling that they, in common with himself, felt a deep and sincere interest in the fate of their missing countrymen. If the work possesses no other merit, it may at least be relied on as the production of one who neglected no opportunity of making himself thoroughly acquainted with the regions he visited, who kept a truthful journal of every event and circumstance at all worthy of record, and who at least had no crotchet or theory to advance or serve. His own opinions are not favourable to the sanguine hopes entertained by many of Sir John Franklin's safety; but the Editor would still draw the attention of the reader to the fact, that if his author is not hopeful, he is not obstinately opposed to the possibility of Franklin's having ascended towards the great Arctic Ocean (if there is one) by way of Wellington Channel or by way of Jones's or Smith's Sound.

Sir Edward Belcher's Expedition will, it is to be hoped, be more successful than that which sailed now three years ago under the command of Captain Austin, and throw some light on the route which was taken by the missing ships after leaving their winter-quarters in Beechey Island. It is at least remarkable that no *further* trace of any kind should have been discovered. As a simple question of evidence, it may be fairly considered as weighing in favour of the presumption that some powerful inducement to take advantage of a sudden opening in the ice had rendered a precipitate movement necessary; and it may also be observed, that at that early period of the expedition Sir John Franklin would not have had any very particular

object in leaving behind him such distinct traces of
his future movements, as seems to have been expected and assumed by the various expeditions in
search of him.   The total destruction of the ships
and crews by the Esquimaux is too improbable even
to command a passing thought.   Masses of ice
might, it is true, have destroyed the vessels, but
then where are the crews?   In such a region it is
not likely that they would have been annihilated by
the same cause.   Starvation and disease may have
overtaken them; but then some traces, like those
of the Patagonian mission, would in all probability
have been found.   On the whole, when the facts
that are known are viewed simply and calmly in
connection with probabilities, and as mere matter
of evidence, it is neither rash, wanton, nor ill-judged,
to foster hopes which, however doomed to be dis-
appointed, are still fairly within the bounds of rea-
sonable probability.

CONTENTS.

FRANKLIN'S FOOTSTEPS.

CHAPTER I.

EARLY ARCTIC EXPEDITIONS.

In the interminable pine-forests and rocky fiords of the North there was much calculated to attract the restless imagination, and excite the wild spirit of adventure, so characteristic of those northern warriors who in a short time overran the whole of western Europe, infusing hardihood and vigour into the effeminate races of the South. The strange admixture of the sublime and terrible in the stern unbending landscape of those ice-bound regions had peculiar charms for men to whom danger was a pastime, and whose religion was one of fear rather than of love. To its influence also we may trace most of that beautiful poetry which remains in the Sagas of the Skalds, and which even to this day is justly esteemed for the richness of its imagery and the lofty grandeur of its expression.

B

Far and near those famous Sea Kings of the
North spread the terror of their arms; there were
few countries in the then known world that had
not felt their power. Not content with scouring the
ocean from the deep fiords of Norway to the warm
seas of Spain and Italy, they turned the prows of
their frail barks northward, and, unassisted by the
compass, yet scorning to creep timidly along the
coast like the more southern navigators, boldly·
plunged into the unknown and ice-encumbered
ocean, and entered the Arctic Regions. Thus
Flokko, a renowned pirate, following the track of
a still more ancient hero, Naddok, settled in a land
surrounded by frozen seas and covered with lofty
mountains, A.D. 864.

At that time Norway was governed by Jarls, or
Earls, under a system nearly allied to our Heptarchy
in England; but at length the whole country was
brought under subjection by King Harold Haafager.
Many of the nobles however, disdaining to yield
their liberties, migrated to more favoured lands.
Ingulf, with his brother-in-law Horlief, led his followers to the Snowland or Iceland of Flokko, and
there established a free republic, A.D. 874.

The flower of the Norman nobility either accompanied Ingulf or settled in the less distant Ferroe
Islands; but the daring Rollo, driven from his
native land by Haafager, and sailing with a chosen
band of nobles, the ancestry of men whose names em-
bellish every page of England's history, conquered

Neustria, and reinvigorated with fresh blood the exhausted and enfeebled Southrons. Ingulf and his Norman colony carried with them to Iceland the Sagas and the stately mythology of their old country. Odin still ruled their longed-for heaven, with his mighty sons, Vali and Balder. These still incited their warlike youth in battle, while Scandinavian literature was preserved in all its fulness by Icelandic bards.

Among the restless spirits who followed Ingulf to Iceland, was Thorwald, a rich and powerful jarl, whose son, Eric Raüde, having slain a neighbouring jarl in a duel, was sentenced to three years' banishment; embarking in a small open vessel, he directed his course westwards, and landed on the granite cliffs of an unknown continent. There he remained during three years of danger and hardship, the period of his banishment, and thus became the discoverer of Greenland, A.D. 982.

Returning to Iceland, he spread such brilliant reports of this newly-discovered land, which he called Engroënland, that, in the following year, twenty-five vessels of colonists assembled under his command, with a view to establish themselves in this favoured country; but such were the fearful dangers of the Northern Ocean, with its huge masses of moving ice, that only fourteen ever reached their destination. More however speedily followed, until both the east and west sides of Greenland became colonized by these valorous sons of the North.

In the year of our Lord 999, Leif, the son of
Eric Raüde, went to the court of Olaus Tryggeson,
king of Norway, who was then endeavouring to
spread the doctrines of the Christian faith with all
the zeal of a recent proselyte; and having wintered
there, Leif returned to Greenland accompanied by
a priest, who succeeded in bringing the first Arctic
colonists into the fold of Christ.

The enterprising spirit of these Northmen, which
had received so great a stimulus by the peopling
of Iceland, Greenland, and the Ferroe Islands, was
now at its height. Many wealthy Icelanders staked
their fortunes on discovery, and amongst others,
Biom, the son of Hergulf, being driven by contrary
winds to the southward, in the year 1001, landed
on a low coast, overgrown with wood. Returning
to Greenland, his story attracted the attention of
the adventurous Leif, who, in the following year,
sailed in the same direction with thirty chosen
men. After a prosperous voyage, they landed on
the same kind of low land covered with wood, and
ascended a noble river, probably the St. Lawrence,
which abounded in all kinds of fish. They had
discovered America: nearly five hundred years before the birth of Columbus the persevering Northmen had set foot on the New World; and there
are proofs that the great navigator himself was well
aware of their discovery.

The romantic tales of this new country led
Thorwald. the brother of Leif, to proceed on another

expedition in the following year; but after having
established himself on a wooded island, he was
killed in a skirmish with the natives (who, on account of their dwarfish stature, were called Skrælings), and was buried with a wooden cross at the
head and foot of his grave,—the first Christian
whose bones found a resting-place in the soil of the
New World.

Several expeditions followed, but all met with
disaster, and by degrees the colony of Vinland
almost sank into oblivion. It is true however that
in A.D. 1121 Eric, Bishop of Greenland, is said to
have gone on a visitation to this distant part of his
see; but the colony gradually became less known,
and was at last completely lost sight of. Many of the
old Norman colonists were probably still heathen,
and, as no intercourse was kept up, they became
in the lapse of years so mixed up with the abori-
gines, that all trace of them was swept away.

Meanwhile Greenland increased in prosperity,
and in A.D. 1122 Sigurd, king of Norway, appointed
Arnold bishop of this Arctic Christian fold, and
suffragan to the archbishop of Drontheim. On arriving there in A.D. 1123, he fixed his episcopal residence at Gardar, where a flourishing colony soon
sprang up, and continued to advance in prosperity,
until the year 1023, when it became tributary to
Norway; from A.D. 1261 it was governed by a regal
deputy, in conjunction with the bishop.

It was in the latter part of the fourteenth cen-

tury that the Skrælings or Esquimaux, mentioned
before as having been seen in Vinland by the sons
of Eric Raüde, are said to have first made their
appearance in Greenland; and from this period the
history of the Norman colony becomes very obscure.
The separate existence of the Normans, the descendants of those doughty knights who spread civilization over every country in which they settled,
had ceased; and the communication between Greenland and the mother country, either by means of
the daring rover, or the more peaceful, though not
unarmed, merchantman, gradually became less frequent, until at last this sterile Arctic coast was
entirely forgotten.

Such, in a few words, is the remarkable history
of Norman Arctic discovery,—of that career of bold
adventure which led the daring sons of the North
from the deep fiords of Norway to the perilous seas
of Greenland, and at length to achieve the discovery of the fertile shores of the St. Lawrence.
It now only remains briefly to recount the same
determined perseverance in Arctic research which
manifested itself at a later period, though previous
to that which forms the chief object of this little
work.

The desire of gain, or of wide-spread fame, has
usually been the urging motive which has sent
forth bold adventurers in all ages, and there is
little in this respect that distinguishes the so-called
days of chivalry from those of commerce.   It was

in the fourteenth century that the Portuguese performed their wondrous deeds in India and China; that the Conquistadores of Spain astonished the world by their vast discoveries and conquests; and that the British heroes of the Elizabethan age led their dauntless followers to the long-neglected shores of the Arctic regions. Violence and cruelty, it is well known, disgraced the track of the conquerors of India and of the New World; and little less can be said for our own navigators, who unscrupulously attacked the vessels of other nations which they met with in those frozen seas. It was the spirit of the age—an age of great deeds performed by lawless means—which tainted every European nation; and it must be confessed that the government which sanctioned the piracies of Drake and Cavendish cannot with justice be excepted. The principal motive however was a laudable one (the desire of reaching China by a shorter route, and thus increasing the commercial prosperity of England), which led the old navigators of this period to steer their course towards the polar sea. For nearly two hundred years the coast of Greenland had remained unvisited—from the time, in fact, that the Norman colonies became extinct to the year 1575, when Sir Martin Frobisher reached a land which he describes as rising like "pinnacles of steeples, and all covered with snow," in N. lat. 61°, and which was evidently the south coast of Greenland. Sir Martin was soon followed by Master John

Davis, who, in the year 1585, arrived on the same
coast, and anchored in a fiord near Cape Farewell.
In 1587 he penetrated still further, reaching that
bold and picturesque mass of granite to which he
gave the name of "Hope Saunderson;" he succeeded also in crossing the straits which bear his
name, where the discoveries of this great navigator
concluded.

A more solid motive however than the mere discovery of unknown countries began at this time to
actuate the English voyagers to the North, and a
cargo of whale-oil amply repaid the first venture of
the merchant. Mr. Jonas Pool may be considered
the founder of the northern whale-fisheries. In
his various voyages he reported having seen so
many whales, and indeed brought home so many
tuns of oil, that the curiosity as well as cupidity
of the whole country was aroused; for this fishery
seemed to open out a field of exhaustless specu-
lation, as well as of almost certain profit. Others
followed with various success, but none of these
gained so much credit as Master F. Edge, who was
sent out by the Muscovite Company in the year
1613. In the meantime attempts at discovering a
North-west Passage were not abandoned, and it is
wonderful with what energy the merchant adventurers of the seventeenth century sought to achieve
a shorter route to Cathay and China. Not the least
among these enterprising men was the intrepid
seaman Baffin, who owes his fame not so much to

his vast terrestrial discoveries as to his great ability
in nautical astronomy ; for Baffin was not only the
discoverer of the mode of finding the longitude by
lunar observation, but he was the first to make
use of astronomical observations with any degree
of accuracy.

In the year 1616 Baffin sailed from Gravesend
on board the ' Discovery,' of fifty-five tons, with
the simple orders to " pass through the north-west
passage, touch at Japan, and so return."   On the
30th of May, Hope Saunderson, the extreme point
reached by Davis, was passed, and Baffin was the
first Englishman to land on that archipelago of islands which has since become so great a resort for
whalers.   Here some Esquimaux were found ; and it
is an important fact, that at the present day the most
northern Esquimaux settlements (with the exception of the Arctic Highlanders) are at Opernavik,
on the opposite shore of Greenland.   These were
the most northern beings seen by Baffin, who, passing with some difficulty through the ice-fields of
Melville Bay, reached a latitude of 78° north, in
Sir Thomas Smith's Sound, where he found the va-
riation of the needle to be 56° west.   Skirting the
western shores of the extensive bay that bears his
name, Baffin concluded this, the most successful of
the Arctic expeditions of the period : he arrived at
Dover on the 30th of August, A.D. 1616.

Two interesting Arctic voyages, though not in
the direction of Baffin's Bay, add an important

feature to northern maritime adventure in the seventeenth century; and one of these expeditions, which passed a winter on the frozen shores of Hudson's Bay, was the first to perform that perilous and hardy feat.

Luke, commonly called North-west, Fox, and Captain James, sailed in 1631 for the Arctic Regions. Fox entered Hudson's Bay in June, and penetrating to that point which has ever since been called "N. W. Fox his furthest," returned to England after an absence of six months. Not so Captain James; he left England in the 'Henrietta Maria' of seventy tons, and made Greenland on the 4th of June; but encountering many and serious disasters, he was eventually forced to winter at Charlton Island, in Hudson's Bay. In this forlorn position the first mishap was the fatal illness of the gunner to the expedition, who begged in his dying moments to be allowed to drink a glass of sack; but " the wine froze in the bottle, as well as the plaster at his wound." Captain James contrived to build a house on shore for wintering in, but so intense was the cold that the men's noses, cheeks, and hands were frozen white as paper : blisters were thus raised as large as walnuts, and both oil and vinegar were hard like pieces of wood. But, what was more mortifying than all the rest, they found, that after getting over the severe winter, April was the coldest month : some of the men had " aches, others sore mouths, insomuch that the surgeon cut away the flesh from their gums every morning, and thus they went through their miseries." Their diet consisted of porridge for breakfast, pork and peas for dinner, and beef which had been boiled in this porridge for supper; Alicant wine was kept for the sick. After a long and dreary winter, during which Captain James exhibited great courage, energy, and endurance, the 'Henrietta Maria' was extricated from the ice on the 2nd of July, and arrived at Bristol in October 1632. This voyage is particularly interesting, as being one of the first in which an Arctic winter was endured and faithfully recorded, and does honour to the gallant seaman who conducted it.

The voyages of Hudson,—which have immortalized his name, and opened the fur-trade of the wilds of North America,—of Waymouth, Willoughby, Button, Hall, and others of less importance, though not immediately connected with our subject, all show with what indomitable perseverance these navigators prosecuted their search for unknown lands. Like their Norman predecessors they fearlessly braved all the hardships of an Arctic climate, with no knowledge of the requisites for passing through the ordeal of a winter; and, like them, they opened a wide field for the enterprise of their successors. Frobisher discovered the continent of Greenland; Hudson's discoveries led the way to the establishment of the fur company, which extends its influence over so large a portion of

North America; Davis and Baffin opened the way
to a lucrative whale-fishery; and the names and
exploits of these great men have added a bright
page to the history of British energy, science, and
adventurous spirit, which has not been surpassed
even by the subsequent achievements of Franklin,
Parry, and Ross.

Having brought down the account of Arctic
discovery to the middle of the last century, it will
not be amiss to say a few words on the Greenland
Settlements themselves, the history of which is little
more than a relation of the difficulties that have
been undergone by those who endeavoured to sow
the seed of Christianity among the wretched natives
who surrounded them. It is sometimes found that
pure philanthropy will induce a high-souled man
to forsake the comforts and conveniences of civilized life, and, actuated by religious zeal and the desire of propagating a sublime and holy creed, to
brave every kind of hardship and danger. Such
a man was Hans Egede, a clergyman of Vogen in
Norway, who, hearing of the wretched state of the
Greenlanders, moral and physical, was induced to
exert himself for their benefit; after fruitlessly
striving for ten years to awaken a similar zeal
among his countrymen, he at length induced the
King to sanction his undertaking a mission to
Greenland. Accompanied by his wife and four
children, with forty other persons, this disinter-
ested man sailed from Bergen in 1721, and after

a tempestuous voyage arrived at Baals river on the west coast of Greenland, and founded the Danish colony of Godhaab in N. lat. 64°. After vainly endeavouring to discover the long-lost Norman colony on the east of Greenland, he, with his companion Albert Top, commenced in good earnest to learn the language and attempt the conversion of the Esquimaux. This work was however very slow, being constantly interrupted and thwarted by the determined opposition of the Augekoks, or Esquimaux priests. These mortifications, added to famine, disease, and the rigour of the seasons, would have reduced a weaker mind to despair; but Hans Egede was not so easily overcome, and in spite of the horrors and misery that met his sight on every side, he, like Pizarro on the Isle of Gorgona, formed the resolution of remaining among the sterile rocks of Greenland, with his ten surviving companions, rather than forsake the duties he had undertaken. This noble endurance soon met with its reward; and it occasioned no slight joy in the colony to hear that the Moravian brethren, on being informed of the exertions of Hans Egede, had sent out missionaries to assist him in his holy work. These men were Christian David, Matthew Stack, and Christian Stack; and it is difficult to conceive the sacrifices these devoted Moravians must have made, in relinquishing the comforts of a happy German home, to minister to the wretched Esquimaux.

Their ordinary difficulties were of course no less

than those endured with so much fortitude by
Egede and his companions; but, to add to their
sufferings, a virulent small-pox broke out among
the natives and carried them off by thousands, so
that the country was well-nigh depopulated round
the lately established settlement of New Herrn-
huth; but even this great calamity did not stagger
the missionaries in their enterprise to reclaim the
remaining heathens.   From year to year their privations were so great that two of them determined
to return home, but Matthew Stack, Frederick
Bæmish, and John Beck declared that nothing
should induce them to forsake their call, and that,
come life, come death, they would remain among
the rocks of Greenland : "The Lord our God can
preserve us," said they; "and if he is not pleased
to do it, we shall fall into his hands."   The vene-
rable Hans Egede, with his devoted wife, had shared
the sufferings of the Moravian missionaries up to
this time, taught them the Esquimaux language,
and encouraged them under their greatest distress.
His faithful partner however, a true heroine, devoted to her husband and to the holy cause for
which he had sacrificed so much, died in the winter
of 1735 ; and in the following spring, Hans Egede
himself, overwhelmed by this addition to his cala-
mities, resolved to leave the scenes of his almost
fruitless toil and return to die in his native land;
he chose for the text of his farewell sermon, the 4th
verse of the 49th chapter of Isaiah : "Then I said,

I have laboured in vain, I have spent my strength
for nought and in vain; yet surely my judgement is
with the Lord, and my work with my God." We
may search the annals of many an empire, and not
find a truer hero than this devoted missionary.

After the departure of Hans Egede little progress
was made. The Esquimaux were stupid, ignorant,
and hardened; those who came from a distance
soon forgot what they heard, and the natives
around Baals river listened with careless inatten-
tion; still the missionaries lost none of their energy, and down to the year 1767 they were un-
remitting in their endeavours to improve both the
physical and spiritual welfare of those among whom
they laboured. At this time the number of Esquimaux converts in the three Moravian settlements was 998; subsequent to that period however
they have somewhat diminished, owing to the mor-
tality which prevents any increase in the population
of this Arctic country, since the introduction of
vices and diseases, incident, it might almost be said,
to civilization.

The most southern Danish settlement is at Fre-
derickshaab, established in 1742. The colonies of
Holsteinborg, Leifly in Disco, and the most northern one, Opernavik, where there is a plumbago-
mine, have all been established by Danish merchants, as depôts for collecting furs, oil, and skins,
which are annually conveyed to Copenhagen.
These settlements are inhabited in a great measure

by a mongrel population; for there can be little
doubt that the pure Danes, who established themselves there from time to time, have in many in-
stances intermarried with the natives, and greatly
improved their physical condition; while the labours
of the worthy Danish and Moravian missionaries
have widely diffused spiritual instruction among
the Esquimaux; it is to be hoped that eventually
by the admixture of European blood the original
stock will disappear and be replaced by a finer race
of men.

CHAPTER II.

GREENLAND WHALE FISHERY.

THE first people who attempted the capture of the whale are supposed to have been the fishermen on the shores of Biscay. Whales were frequently stranded on the beach, and considerable profit was realized by the sale of the bone and blubber; so valuable indeed did these occasional prizes prove, that in a short time a band of adventurous fishermen fitted out a small craft, for the purpose of attacking and capturing the leviathan of the deep. Their success inspired others, until few fishing-vessels from these parts put to sea without some rude weapons, to enable them to contend with such of these monsters as chance should throw in their way.

It has been seen how successful were the fishing voyages of Master Jonas Pool and Master Edge in the beginning of the seventeenth century: these men were, in fact, the fathers of the English whale-

c

fishery; but, for many years subsequent to their
return, the Dutch and other nations far surpassed
us in the success of their ventures.   The first enterprise of the Dutch in this fishery was in the
year 1612, in the deep bays of Spitzbergen, where
whales abounded; and during the seventeenth century this branch of trade increased so rapidly, that
a regular town, afterwards called Smeerenberg,
arose on the island of Amsterdam (Spitzbergen).
Three hundred vessels annually frequented the
surrounding bays, traders of every kind resorted
thither, and for years it was looked upon by the
States General as another Batavia.

From 1630 to 1640 however, the whales, having
been harassed for many years, at length began to
retreat from the coasts to the open sea; Smeerenberg was therefore gradually deserted; the blubber,
instead of being landed and boiled down on the
shore, was then merely packed in casks, and conveyed to Holland: in 1770 the Dutch whale-fishery
began sensibly to decline, and in 1795 there were
only sixty Dutch whalers.

The English meanwhile had, in their fishing
enterprises, met with repeated failures.   In 1635
Charles I. ceded the whale-fishery to the Russia
Company, but so little use was made of this grant,
that the trade can hardly be said to have existed
until 1725, when the South Sea Company sent
twelve ships to Greenland; they however abandoned it in 1737.

In the middle of the last century the whale-fishery began again to assume some importance, and in 1756 it was generally successful. In 1787 thirty-one ships sailed from Scotland, and returned with 84 whales and 6571 seals, yielding 1274 tuns of blubber. Two hundred whalers sailed from England at the same period.

About this time also the Hull vessels discovered the volcanic island of Jan Mayen, around which the fishing continued to be very successful; and from 1813 to 1818, 68,940 tuns of oil and 3420 tons of whalebone were imported into England.

The fishery on the west coast of Greenland was not commenced until a much later date than the fisheries in the seas around Spitzbergen, Jan Mayen, and East Greenland. The Davis's Straits fishery was first opened by the Dutch in 1719, after which time nearly half their whalers yearly resorted to the bays and fiords of Greenland,— South Bay, in 66° 30′ N., being their usual rendez-vous. The English soon followed them, but it was long before they had the hardihood to force their way through the northern barriers of ice, and, following in the track of Baffin, enter the open water of the bay which bears his name. That clear-headed navigator saw the profit that would accrue from the Baffin's Bay fishery, at least two centuries before any attempt was made to realize the advantages he pointed out. In his letter to Sir John Wolstenholme, on the return of his successful expedition in 1619, he speaks thus :—" And first, for killing of whales : certaine it is, that in this bay are great numbers of them, which the Biscainers call the grand baye whales, of the same kind which are killed at Greenland, and, as it seemeth to me, easie to be strooke, because they are not used to be chased or beaten ; for we, being but one day in Whale's Sound, so called from the number of whales that we saw there, sleeping and lying aloft on the water, not fearing our ship or ought else, that if we had beene fitted with men and things necessarie, it had beene no hard matter to have stroke more than would have made these ships a saving voyage."

It was not until 1817 (the year before the first modern Arctic expedition sailed) that two or three English whalers ventured to sail up Baffin's Bay, where, in July and August, they found the sea abounding in whales. In the following year several other vessels passed the barrier of ice between 74° and 75° north latitude, and found a navigable sea in the northern part of the bay, formed by the drifting of the ice to the southward, and which has usually been called the North Water. Since that time a fleet of whalers have annually resorted thither, passing the barrier if possible in the beginning of July, and going south along the west coast of Baffin's Bay. Of late years the whales have not been so numerous, for, having been disturbed and actively pursued for a length of time, they have changed their place of resort; and consequently the number of whaling ships in these seas is now much less than formerly.

The whalers in Baffin's Bay are usually of 300 to 400 tons burden, very strong and well fortified against the ice. The crews, consisting of from forty to fifty men, are lodged in berths, each calculated to contain three persons. In the rigging of a whaler, great attention is paid to the adaptation of purchases, and enabling her to be worked with as few hands as possible; for it often happens that the greater part of the crew are away in the boats, and three or four men have to tack a ship of 300 tons.

The crow's-nest is another peculiarity in the whalers: this was invented by Captain Scoresby, the famous whaling-master, and first used in 1807. When the vessel is surrounded by floating masses of ice, it is necessary to have a man constantly stationed on the look-out, at the mast-head. The sharp winds, frequently charged with minute particles of frozen vapour, cut his face most painfully, until a cylindrically-shaped pent-house was invented, formed of wooden hoops and covered with painted canvas, with a trap-door in the bottom; this is lashed to the top-gallantmast-head, and enables the ice-master to look out in comfort: from its position and form it is called the crow's-nest.

The boats of a whaler hang from davits all round her, from abreast of the foremast to the

stern.   They are always carver-built, with the
bow and stern both sharp, and the keel depressed
some inches in the middle, to allow of her turning
more easily.   The six-oared boats are twenty-six
to twenty-eight feet long, and five feet nine inches
broad.

The crew of a whaler receives a gratuity for
each fish besides his monthly pay.   The master
and each harpooner receive, instead of wages, a certain sum before starting, and if the ship returns
with no cargo they get nothing more.   The master
is usually paid three guineas for each whale, and
10s. per tun of oil; each harpooner receives half-a-
guinea per whale, and 6s. per tun of oil; the chief
mate two guineas a month whilst at sea, and a
guinea for each fish; the specksioneer, or chief harpooner, 10s. 6d. per fish; and the boat-steerers,
line-managers, and foremast-men have each 1s. 6d.
per tun.

The vessels usually sail from Hull, Peterhead,
Aberdeen, or Dundee, in the beginning of March;
and those engaged in the seal-trade proceed at
once northward, meeting the ice in about lat. 72°;
as the season advances they try for whales, which
are usually most plentiful in June.

When a whale is seen from the crow's-nest, a
boat is immediately sent in pursuit, provided with
two harpoons and six or eight lances; the crew
consists of a steerer, a harpooner, a line-manager,
and four rowers.   The harpooner commands and

pulls the bow-oar, while the line-manager takes stroke; the steerer looks out, and gives notice to the harpooner when near enough. The harpoon is a barbed dart three feet long, with a socket at the blunt end, into which a handle is fitted. A piece of 2-inch*, four fathoms long, is spliced round the shank of the harpoon, called the "foreganger," which is fastened to the handle, and keeps it in its place until the harpoon is thrown; the handle then falls out, and the dart sticks firmly into the body of the whale.

The harpoon-gun, now generally employed, was invented in 1731, but fell into disuse for many years. It is a swivel-gun, fitted in the bows of the boat, about twenty-four inches long, and the bore $1\frac{1}{2}$-inch in diameter; the shank of the harpoon terminates in a cylindrical knob, fitting the bore; a ring, to which the line is attached, works on the shank, but remains at the muzzle until the gun is fired, when it flies back to the knob.

The whale-lines are 120 fathoms long, and $2\frac{1}{2}$-inch; they are spliced together, six for each boat, and coiled down in racks.

When struck the whale immediately dives, taking the line with him, which flies out at a tremendous pace. The harpooner usually takes a turn or two round the bollard† to impede the rush of the

---

* Rope is called 1-inch, $2\frac{1}{2}$-inch, etc., according to its circumference.

† A block of wood, fixed firmly in the bows of the boat.

whale as much as possible; even then the line runs
out at such a rate that he is surrounded with
smoke by the friction, and it would inevitably set
the boat on fire, if the wood of the bollard were
not well seasoned.   Meanwhile a flag is put up in
the boat, which gives notice to the ship that the
whale is struck; the instant this signal is seen, the
crew rush to the boats, and if it is night, the excitement is such that they jump out of their berths
and fly on deck with their clothes in their hands,
not to lose a moment in unnecessary preparation.

The boats leave the ship, and assemble near the
place where the whale is expected to rise.   If it is
at the edge of a field of ice, he usually dives under
it obliquely, and comes up exhausted at the edge,
where it is attacked with lances about six feet long,
and killed.

The exhaustion of the whale, on rising, is caused
not so much by the harpoon, as by the great pressure he undergoes in the almost unfathomable
depths to which he has penetrated.   The area of a
large whale is 1540 square feet, so that at a depth
of 800 fathoms he undergoes a pressure of 211,200
tons*.

When the whale is dead, the boats take him in
tow, and bring him alongside the ship, ready for
flensing†.

The common Greenland whale (*Balæna mysti-*

---

* Thirty-five cubic feet of water weighing one ton.
† Flensing is taking off the fat and whalebone.

cetus) is the largest animal in creation. Its length varies from forty-five to sixty feet, and its circumference, in the broadest part, is from thirty to forty feet. The enormous mouth, when open, is ten or twelve feet high and sixteen long, of sufficient size indeed to allow a large boat to sail into it. There are two fins, nearer the snout than the tail, which is six feet long and twenty-six wide. On the top of the head are the spiracles, or blow-holes, which are longitudinal apertures six inches long. The colour of the skin is velvet-black, grey, and white, and the blubber, which lies between the cuticle and the flesh, is generally from ten to twenty inches in thickness. The whalebone serves as a substitute for teeth, and is composed of three hundred laminæ on each side of the head; the greatest length is fifteen feet, and the breadth ten inches.

The whale is now secured by a purchase called the "kent-purchase," which is made fast to the mainmast-head, the other end being hooked to the kent, or fat of the neck. The fall is hauled taut at the windlass, and the fish raised some inches out of the water.

After the men have refreshed themselves, the harpooners get on the whale, under the direction of the specksioneer, while two boats attend alongside. They first divide the fat into oblong pieces by means of blubber-spades, and then flay these off, by hauling on a small tackle inboard. The boat-steerers and line-managers receive the blubber

on deck in pieces of about half a ton each, and
pass them down to be packed in the hold.   The
fat being taken from the belly, the fish is turned by
means of the kent-tackle : the lip is then opened,
and the whalebone dislodged.   The whole of the
blubber and whalebone being taken, the carcase
is cast adrift, and instantly attacked by thousands
of voracious gulls of all descriptions.

The great difficulty of the Baffin's Bay whalers
consists in passing the barrier of ice, which begins
a little to the north of Upernavik and extends to
Cape York.   The loss of one or more of these vessels is of almost yearly occurrence, from their being
pressed, or " nipped," between two fields of ice.
There is something peculiarly striking in the sight
of a fleet of whalers lying motionless at the edge
of the ice, when a large moving floe * drifts down
upon them, threatening them all with instant destruction.

When surrounded in this manner, and in danger
of being completely jammed up, the crews leave the
ship, and proceed to cut a dock in the ice, with ice-
saws.   These are about fourteen feet long, and fitted
with wooden triangles, each of them being attached
to a rope, which, passing through a block in the
triangle, and dividing into *bell-ropes,* is worked by
almost any number of men.   This business is ac-

---

* A *floe* is a piece of ice, of great extent, but the end of which
is visible,—in contradistinction to a *field,* which reaches to the
horizon.

companied by singing, and is perhaps the liveliest
scene in the whole voyage.   When the dock is
cleared, the ships enter, and are for the time safe
from the ice, which however has been known to
come with such force as to break up the floe in
which the docks are cut, piling up immense masses
of ice, in every variety of shape, over the bows of
the whalers, and overwhelming them.

But the most fearful danger is that of being
forced to winter in these Arctic regions without
requisite preparation.   Unable to escape from the
surrounding masses of ice, the crew of the ill-fated
vessel behold their companions getting clear one
by one, until they are left in their icy cradle, to
pass a dreary winter, with the icebergs towering up
around them, and a death-like stillness prevailing
over everything, only broken occasionally by the
crash of some huge block in falling—

" Cæruleâ glacie concretæ atque imbribus atris."

The whaling fleet however usually returns home in
the months of September and October.

Such is a slight sketch of the perils which menace
the Arctic whalers.   There is however a charm
about the wild adventures and magnificent scenery
in Baffin's Bay, and an excitement in the chase of
the whale, the cutting of docks, and the hair-breadth
escapes from destruction, which seldom fails to cap-
tivate the rough seamen engaged in it.   Many of
them have been thirty and forty voyages, and many

more end their lives and are buried on some, barren
island, amid the fantastic icebergs and the screech-
ing sea-birds.   The neat head-board carved by a
friendly hand tells the short and melancholy tale,
while the eider-duck frequently keeps watch over
the dead by building her downy nest on the grave*

---

* On one of the granite Vrow Islands is the grave of a whale-
fisherman, covered over with moss, in which, above his breast,
an eider-duck had formed her nest, containing two eggs.—July,
1851.

CHAPTER III.

MODERN ARCTIC EXPEDITIONS.

THE Arctic regions have for ages attracted the attention of the learned and adventurous. Impelled by various motives, the energy of almost every maritime nation in Europe has, from time to time, been directed towards the discovery of those hidden lands or seas which, in the most northern parts of the frigid zone, are hemmed in by almost impenetrable barriers of ice.

We have seen how the valorous Normans of old crossed the stormy Atlantic, and reached the shores of Greenland and America; how the brave old seamen of our Elizabethan age explored the unknown regions of Davis's Strait and Baffin's Bay; how the fearless Danish and German missionaries established themselves among the barren rocks of a frozen continent; and how eagerly English seamen risk their lives in the whale-fishery amid the perils of an ice-encumbered sea. In our

own time however a different motive has induced
England to make her gigantic, and partially successful, attempts at Arctic discovery.

At the general peace in 1815, public attention became gradually directed to the subject of discovery
and the advancement of science; and when it was
reported by Scoresby and others that during the
years 1815, 1816, and 1817, there had been a
great clearance of ice in the Arctic regions, Sir
John Barrow and Sir Joseph Banks promoted the
equipment of an expedition in search of a North-
west Passage through Baffin's Bay.

In May, 1818, Captain Ross sailed on this adventurous voyage with two vessels, the 'Alexander'
and 'Isabella,' and reached the northern part of
the island of Disco on the 17th of June. After encountering great difficulty in passing through the
barrier of ice usually extending between Cape York
and the Devil's Thumb,—which line of coast was
called Melville Bay,—the expedition arrived off the
north-west part of that bay, the coast of which is
covered with an enormous glacier, reaching in many
places to the sea. Here Captain Ross fell in with
a tribe of Esquimaux, whom he called "Arctic
Highlanders,"—the most northern inhabitants of
the world. They had sledges and dogs, but no
canoes, and appeared to be in a more wretched condition than their southern brethren.

This is the only interesting event in the voyage.
Leaving the west coast of Baffin's Bay, an optical

illusion prevented the ships discovering the entrance to those magnificent straits which form the
outlets to its northern shore; and this expedition,
barren in all practical results, returned to England
in the month of November, 1818.

Unsatisfactory however as was the first modern
Arctic expedition, the thirst for discovery was not
discouraged by the failure of one commander; and
in the following year Lieutenant Parry, who had
commanded the 'Alexander,' fitted out another
expedition, consisting of the 'Hecla,' 375 tons, and
'Griper,' 180 tons, to explore the North-west Passage by way of Lancaster Sound.

On the 11th of May, 1819, the expedition sailed
from England, and on the 4th of August, after a
prosperous voyage, entered the sound, and *passed
over the mountains* which to Sir John Ross's vision
had unfortunately stopped further progress in that
direction.   What must have been the feeling of
these enterprising voyagers, when they found themselves sailing with a fresh breeze down an entirely
unknown strait, bounded by perpendicular cliffs
never before beheld by European eye, and with
every prospect of performing that voyage which had
baffled the attempts of centuries!   This strait was
called after Sir John Barrow, the great promoter
of Arctic discovery.

There is something calculated to strike the mind
with reverential awe in first entering upon an unknown region.   The perpendicular cliffs of Bar-

row's Strait are composed of dark limestone, and
the streams of melted snow falling from their sum-
mits have, in the course of time, worked deep
fissures, which make the intermediate buttresses
stand out in bold relief, and assume the extraordinary appearance of a succession of columns rising
from the sea in frowning majesty, and support-
ing the blue vault of heaven on their snow-covered
architrave.   Every eye was directed with intense
eagerness to the westward, and great was the
disappointment when a line of ice was observed
extending to the north from Leopold Island, and
closely packed.   A broad opening to the south
was called by Parry "Prince Regent's Inlet," and
was explored as far south as 72° 13′ north, where
a compact barrier of ice was found to stretch from
shore to shore.   Returning therefore to the northern
coast of Barrow's Strait, the Expedition crossed the
entrance of Wellington Channel, which was clear
of ice as far as the eye could reach, and passed
rapidly to the west.

Many islands were discovered in their progress,
and a line of coast to the northward.   Far to the
south a lofty bluff was seen rising above the horizon, and was named "Cape Walker."   The barren limestone shores of newly discovered land—
Cornwallis, Griffith, Brown, Somerville, Lowther,
Young, Garrett, and Baker Isles,—were passed in
succession; but no boat landed till the Expedition reached the sandstone beach of Byam Martin

Island.   Here the remains of six Esquimaux huts
were found, evidently of great age, but curious
and interesting, as being the first traces of man
observed since the Expedition passed the portals of
Lancaster Sound.

Proceeding westward, Parry crossed the meri-
dian of 110° west, and thus the Expedition became
entitled to a reward of £5000, granted by an Order
in Council*.   They were here stopped by a barrier
of ice, and the young ice began to form so rapidly
that it was found necessary to seek safe winter-
quarters.   The coast to the north, after leaving
Byam Martin Island, had been landed upon several
times, and was called Melville Island; it is composed of sandstone, and, compared with the barren
limestone rocks between this island and Wellington Channel, abounds in moss, and at certain seasons of the year in animal food.   The vessels, after
cutting a canal in the ice more than two miles long,
were on the 23rd of September safely moored in
a winter harbour on the south shore of Melville
Island.

The Arctic winter that ensued was one of extraordinary rigour, (the last deer, many of which
had been killed, was seen on October 17th,) and a
desolate stillness prevailed, occasionally broken by
the laughter-loving audience of an Arctic theatre
on board the Hecla.

As the warmer months advanced, Parry deter-

* Act 58 Geo. III., cap. 20.

D

mined on an attempt to explore the northern shore
of Melville Island.

This was the first travelling party which ever
endured the hardships of the frozen ground and
cutting winds of this latitude at a distance from
the ships.   It is impossible to overrate the importance of travelling parties on foot, both for exploring and searching : more has been done by that
means than will ever be attained by sailing; and
if ever the North-west Passage is discovered in the
latitude, or north, of Melville Island, it is probable that such an exploit will be performed by
overland parties. The first attempt therefore at
this mode of discovery is very interesting.   The
Expedition was equipped in the following manner.

The provisions were carried on a light cart with
two wheels, carrying also two blanket-tents, wood
for fuel, three weeks' provisions, cooking apparatus, ammunition, and three guns,—in all, 800 lbs.
weight.   The allowance per man was one pound of
biscuit, two-thirds of a pound of preserved meat,
one pound of sugar, and one gill of spirits.   Each
person carried, in addition, a blanket bag, and a
haversack containing one pair of shoes, one pair
of stockings, and a flannel shirt,—weighing, in all,
from 18 to 24 lbs. The party left the ships on the
1st of June, and travelled by night, both to prevent
injury to their eyes from the glare of the sun on
the snow, and also to obtain more warmth while
sleeping.   Crossing some vast plains covered with

snow, and several rugged ravines, they reached the sea on the northern shore, and named a distant island Sabine Island, after that celebrated engineering officer who accompanied the Expedition. During this journey the party experienced great assistance in dragging the cart by rigging it with a sail.

Returning south, Parry left some lofty blue hills to the west, and reached a wild, picturesque spot, which was named Bushnan Cove, situated on the shores of a deep gulf penetrating the west coast of Melville Island. This was called Liddon's Gulf. In descending a steep and narrow ravine, the axletree of the cart broke in two, and the wheels were left behind; there they remained until 1851, when Lieutenant M'Clintock met with them on his wonderful journey, and used them for firewood.

Parry's party returned across the land, and arrived at Winter Harbour by the 15th of June, having travelled over an estimated distance of 180 miles, at the rate of twelve miles per day.

Such was the first Arctic travelling party in these latitudes, which, though starting in the warmest month in the year, and remaining but a short time away, accomplished the object for which it was equipped, and discovered land never visited until the late Expedition.

On the 1st of August, the Hecla and Griper, after having been fast locked in their icy harbour*

* The rise and fall of the tide in Winter Harbour was four feet four inches.

for ten months, at length got into clear water, and
again attempted to press onwards to the west; but
an interminable barrier of thick-ribbed ice stopped
their progress; and after naming the extreme west
point visible "Cape Dundas," and a coast-line
clearly seen to the southward "Banks's Land,"
Parry thought it advisable to return to England*.

On the 30th of August the entrance to Prince
Regent's Inlet was found to be blocked up with
ice, and the Expedition re-entered Baffin's Bay and
left the scenes of its interesting discoveries on the
5th of September.

After a very rough passage across the Atlantic,
Parry landed at Peterhead, and concluded one of
the most successful voyages ever attempted in the
Arctic Regions†.

The unsatisfactory conclusion of this, as of every
other voyage in search of a North-west Passage,
induced Captain Parry to advocate a search in the
northern part of Hudson's Bay, and along the
north coast of America; and accordingly two years
and a half (1821–3) were spent in the discovery
of Hecla and Fury Strait, and the adjoining land.
But the unsatisfactory termination of this expedition led Parry again to turn his attention towards
the regions beyond Lancaster Sound, where he

---

* He had only two years' provisions on leaving England.
† The islands from Wellington Channel to Melville Island,
which were at first called the North Georgian Group, have since
been known as the Parry Islands.

had gained his greatest fame; and so strong was the confidence of Government in this distinguished officer, that he again received the command of the Hecla and Fury, which sailed on the 19th of May, 1824.

Disaster attended Parry's third voyage from the very outset. The immense quantity of ice blocking up Baffin's Bay, impeding the progress of the ships, and frequently placing them in the most perilous positions, delayed their entrance into Lancaster Sound until the 10th of September. The season was too far advanced to enable them to proceed much further west; the young ice formed rapidly around them, and it was with great difficulty that on the 27th they reached winter-quarters in Port Bowen, on the east coast of Prince Regent's Inlet.

The dreary winter was enlivened by an amusement quite novel in the history of the Parry Islands. Theatrical entertainments had been given in Winter Harbour, and 'The Rivals,' 'Miss in her Teens,' and 'The Mayor of Garratt,' had been acted on an Arctic stage in 1819–20; but it was left for Captain Hoppner, of the Fury, to propose, and the Arctic Expedition of 1824 to carry out, the first *bal masqué* ever heard of in these regions. It was during the dark and dreary days of an Arctic winter that these performances took place. Port Bowen re-echoed to the joyous laughter of the maskers. The gallant inventor of the amusement kept up the disguise of a one-legged fiddler during a whole evening; and in after years, when his First Lieutenant* commanded the Expedition of 1850-1, the memory of its success induced him to resort to the same pastime, as part of that recreation which is so necessary during the tedious winter months, to keep up the health and spirits of the men.

In the spring of 1825 several travelling parties were despatched in different directions. Captain Hoppner attempted to explore the interior, but the depth and frequency of the ravines rendered his progress slow; two other parties, of four men and an officer, likewise examined and surveyed part of the shore to the north and south of Port Bowen.

On the 20th of July the vessels got clear of their-winter quarters. The huge masses of ice drifted them rapidly down the inlet, and on the 2nd of August the Fury was forced on shore, and on the 21st, being again stranded, she had to be abandoned; the stores and provisions were left in a heap on the beach, and the crew was taken on board the Hecla, which arrived off Sheerness in October.

On the return of Captain Parry, the feasibility of reaching the North Pole attracted the attention of that indefatigable navigator; and in 1827 he was again given the command of the Hecla, to make this bold attempt. Sailing from the Nore

* Captain Horatio Thomas Austin, R.N., C.B.

on April 4th, he anchored in Hecla Cove, Spitzbergen, June 22nd.

On June 24th Parry left the ships, with seventy-one days' provisions, in two boats, named the Enterprise and Endeavour, twenty feet long and seven broad, flat-floored, with a bamboo mast nineteen feet long, tarred duck-sails, steer-oar, fourteen paddles, a spreet, and boathook. Each boat, with stores complete, weighed 3753 lbs., or 268 lbs. per man (two officers and twelve men). There were also four sledges of 26 lbs. each. The allowance per man was 10 oz. of biscuit, 9 oz. of pemmican, 1 oz. of cocoa, 1 gill of rum, and 3 oz. of tobacco per week. The cooking apparatus consisted of an iron boiler over a shallow spirit-lamp with seven wicks, which, with one pint of spirits-of-wine, boiled twenty-eight pints of cocoa in an hour and a quarter.

Owing to their starting too late in the season, the ice was frequently found to be in a state of motion; they had to launch the boats, and then haul them again on to the ice; and sometimes, after travelling all day, they found that they had even lost latitude by the ice drifting south; so that, after enduring great fatigue, they only reached 82° 45' north, and on the 2nd of August returned to the Hecla, having travelled 569 miles during an absence of fifty-seven days*.

* Though this Expedition proved unsuccessful, I conceive the attempt to reach the Pole, provided that it is not surrounded

The next expedition through Lancaster Sound
was a private one, under Captain Ross, who sailed
in the Victory, of 180 tons, fitted with a small
steam-engine and paddles. His object was to set at

by vast mountains of granite, to be by no means impossible.—
If the theory of a polar basin be incorrect, and the regions
around the Pole are imbedded in field-ice during the winter, as
there is every reason to believe, from the quantity of ice Parry
found drifting south, the plan would be to despatch a fully-
equipped Arctic ship, and a strong little Norwegian prawl. The
ship should winter in the Hecla Cove, and the smaller vessel
press on during that season as far as possible, and winter in the
Pack, say in 83° north, or 84°, or, if lucky, 85°. Early in the
ensuing April the whole of the crew which composed her—say
twenty men—should proceed in two parties to the north, having
the Hecla to fall back upon, as their own vessel would probably
have been destroyed or drifted out by the ice before their return.
They should be each equipped for eighty days, with a sledge and
boat. The distance to the Pole would be, from 85° north, only three
hundred miles, or from 84° north, three hundred and sixty miles,
which might be done at ten miles a day, in thirty or thirty-six days,
thus reaching the North Pole long before the ice begins to break
up, and returning by boat and sledge, according to the state of
the ice, to the Hecla. This boat, I conceive, should be flat-floored,
and supported by a strong sledge, with strong runners, and cross-
pieces and bearer to fit the bottom of the boat, and made to take
easily to pieces and stow away. The provisions would be stowed
in a boat, which would easily hold eighty days ; and the men would
sleep on the ice in light tents, or in the boat, covered with tar-
paulin and buffalo-skins. Thus, by wintering far to the northward, the travelling parties would have several hundred miles'
start ; and by leaving their vessel so early (I left Griffith Island
on April 4th) they would be spared the annoyance of being drifted
to the south, until they had reached the Pole, and on their return
it would assist them. If, on the contrary, a Polar basin does
exist, this plan would only be rendered more practicable and less
laborious by using boat and sails.

rest the question of a North-west Passage south of
Barrow's Strait. After a prosperous voyage he entered Prince Regent's Inlet, and having supplied
himself with provisions from the stores abandoned
by the Fury (the vessel herself had entirely disappeared), the Victory proceeded south, and discovered
three hundred miles of new coast-line, which was
called Felix-Boothia*. Captain Ross secured his
vessel in safe winter-quarters in September 1829.
The excursions of his second in command†, assisted by the Esquimaux, enabled him to discover
the North Magnetic Pole‡, in 70° 5′ 17″ north, and
95° 46′ 45″ west, near Cape Nikolai, on the western
shore of Boothia : the amount of the dip was 89° 59′,
being within one minute of the vertical. As the
vessel could not be extricated from the ice, she was
abandoned in 1832, and Captain Ross led his men,
with boats and provisions, to Fury Beach, where a
fourth winter was passed, in a canvas house banked
up with snow. In the following year the boats
were launched, and after many days of hard pulling Captain Ross and his crew were picked up in
Lancaster Sound by a whaler. The question of a
North-west Passage in any direction south of Lan-

* From Sir Felix Booth, an opulent distiller, who assisted the
equipment of the expedition with £17,000, and on its return was
made a baronet by William IV.

† Commander James C. Ross.

‡ The north and south magnetic poles are now supposed to be
centres of magnetic intensity,—*moveable* points, revolving within
the frigid zones.

caster Sound, has been for ever set at rest by this expedition and the recent discoveries of Dr. Rae in Repulse Bay.

The travelling parties of Franklin and Richardson, of Dease, Simpson, and Rae, on the shores of North America, are not sufficiently connected with my subject to be further noticed. There is a wide difference between the fir-clad banks of the Mackenzie or the Coppermine, and the naked rocks of the Parry Islands. Franklin and his brave companions, in the expedition of 1820, were enabled to live on *tripe de roche**, but in the Parry Islands sufficient could not be collected to satisfy one man for a single day. In Repulse Bay even, where no drift-wood is to be found, Dr. Rae used the clubmoss (*Andromeda tetragona*) for fuel; but in the Parry Islands no such useful plant was met with between Melville Island and Cape Warrender.

It is evident therefore that even the shores of Arctic America are not to be compared in desolate wretchedness with those inhospitable regions which lie further north, and that the experience of the one cannot be applied to the other.

Between the return of Sir John Ross, in 1834, and 1845, little was done in the way of Arctic discovery. Whalers indeed are said occasionally to have gone up Barrow's Strait, and even the islands in Wellington Channel seen by the United States Expedition, and marked on the charts as Mr. Penny's

* A species of lichen.

discoveries, were first observed by Mr. Parker, of the 'True Love' whaler; but it was not until the return of Sir John Franklin from the government of Van Diemen's Land, that the attention of Government was again turned toward the Arctic Regions.

At the instigation of Sir John Barrow, two bomb-vessels, the Erebus and the Terror, lately returned from Sir James Ross's Antarctic expedition, with small auxiliary steam-engines and screw-propellers, were fitted out under the command of Sir John Franklin, and sailed from England on May the 26th, 1845.

That gallant officer, who had already suffered so many fearful hardships in Arctic America, was then fifty-nine years old. The expedition consisted of twenty-three officers and one hundred and fifteen men,—in all, one hundred and thirty-eight souls. They arrived at the Whale-fish Islands, a group to the south of Disco, on the 4th of July, and on the 26th were seen moored to an iceberg in 74° 48′ north latitude and 66° 13′ west longitude, by Captain Dannet of the Prince of Wales* (a Hull whaler). They have not been heard of since; and no traces, save the remains of winter-quarters of 1845–6, at Beechey Island, have been discovered.

Their long absence began, in 1847, to excite the apprehension of Government; and in June 1848

* This whaler, with two others, the Superior of Peterhead, and Lady Jane of Newcastle, were lost in Baffin's Bay in 1849.

Sir James Ross, an officer who had accompanied
almost every expedition, both Arctic and Antarctic,
and has been further north and south than any man
living, sailed in search of the missing expedition
with two vessels, the Enterprise and Investigator.

They reached Barrow's Strait in the end of
August, and, owing to the state of the ice, were
forced to winter in Leopold Harbour. During the
following May and June*, Sir James Ross and
Lieutenant M'Clintock explored the whole of the
north and west coasts of North Somerset in two
sledges, with crews of six men each, and returned
to the ships on June 23rd, having been thirty-
nine days absent. During these excursions they
shot seven ducks, eight ptarmigan, one glaucous
gull†, two silver gulls, one kittiwake, three dove-
heys, two boatswains, one red-throated diver, one
snow bunting,—in all, twenty-six birds; they caught
also a lemming, saw three bears, and wounded two
of them. Other parties explored Cape Hurd, Cape
York, and the east shore of North Somerset, as far
as Fury Beach, where Sir John Ross's house and
much of the Fury's provisions still remained. On
the 28th of August the vessels got clear of Leopold Harbour, leaving a wooden house, twelve
months' provisions, fuel, and a small steam-launch,
on Whaler Point. From the 1st to the 25th of

---

* Started May 15th, returned June 23rd,—thirty-nine days.

† Gulls arrive in May; early in June a flock of sandpipers and
the first ducks were seen.

September the vessels were closely beset by the ice, and in the greatest danger of being crushed to pieces, but they eventually drifted into Baffin's Bay, and having at length extricated themselves, reached England in November.

Meanwhile the North Star (an old twenty-six-gun frigate of 500 tons) had sailed from England, with provisions for the Expedition of Sir James Ross, in the spring of 1849, but was forced to winter in Wolstenholme Sound on the west coast of Greenland, after having been sixty-two days in the ice.

Such is a brief account of the first unsuccessful attempts to relieve Sir John Franklin's ships.

CHAPTER IV.

CAPTAIN AUSTIN'S EXPEDITION.

On receiving intelligence of the unsuccessful termination of Sir John Ross's expedition, the Government determined on sending out four more vessels, in the hope of rescuing, or at least of obtaining some information respecting the fate of, the missing vessels.

Captain Austin* was selected, on the recommendation of Sir Edward Parry, to command the new Arctic expedition, consisting of four vessels, which were commissioned on February 28th, 1850. The Resolute, of 410 tons, was a bark built at Shields; the Assistance, commanded by Captain Ommanney,

---

* Captain Austin was first lieutenant of the Fury, in her disastrous voyage to the Arctic Regions, 1824–5. He subsequently served in the Chanticleer (surveying vessel) in the Pacific Ocean, and has since commanded several steamers. He was at the attack and taking of Sidon in 1840. When appointed to command the Arctic expedition, he was Captain of the Blenheim, line-of-battle ship.

of 430 tons (to which the author was appointed),
was built at Bombay by a son of Sir Robert Sep-
pings, the famous naval architect, and had formerly
been a trader in the China Sea; to each vessel
was attached a screw steam-tender of sixty-horse
power, the Intrepid and the Pioneer*. With these
ships the rescue of Sir John Franklin was to be
attempted. The Government also deemed it ex-
pedient to employ two brigs under Mr. Penny, a
whaling captain, to search Jones's Sound; these
were fitted out at Aberdeen; nor would old Sir
John Ross be left behind, but followed in a small
schooner of his own.

Captain Austin's expedition had a supply of provisions for three years, and a transport was to complete it at the Whale-fish Islands. The complement
of each bark was sixty men, and of the tenders thirty,
—in all a hundred and eighty men. No vessels ever
sailed from England with a greater prospect of success: all on board were enthusiastic in the extreme,
and determined to exert their utmost energies and
use all the means in their power to further the noble
cause in which they were engaged; the vast tracts
of country discovered and explored by Captain
Austin's Expedition will remain for ever on the
map of the world a proof of how that determination

* These four vessels were bought by Government. Their
names were changed on the occasion: the Resolute was formerly
the Ptarmigan—the Assistance, the Baboo—the Pioneer, the Ida
—and the Intrepid, the Freetrader. The Resolute was fitted out
by contract by Green, and the Assistance by Wigram.

has been carried out.   We sailed from England on
the 3rd of May, passed Cape Wrath on the 15th, and,
after a prosperous voyage, arrived at the Whale-
fish Islands, a group on the west coast of Greenland, south of Disco, by the 16th of June, where
we were to receive the remainder of our supply of
provisions from the transport*.

* The provisions of H.M.S. Assistance, on leaving England,
were increased one-third at the Whale-fish Islands (except small
stores, milk, chocolate, etc.), being three years' for sixty men, and
two years' salt meat for thirty men, for the tenders, viz.—

Rum (40 over proof) 1455 gall.	Preserved soups .	7,060 lb.
Biscuit . . 21,896 lb.	„ vegetables	9,020 „
Salt beef . . 13,984 „	„ potatoes	4,928 „
Salt pork . . 18,560 „	„ apples .	2,352 „
Flour . . . 56,200 „	Pepper	200 „
Suet . . . . 1,792 „	Mustard . . .	368 „
Currants . . 350 „	Salt	280 „
Peas . . . . 77 bsh.	Dried yeast . .	40 „
Chocolate . . 4,148 lb.	Pemmican . . .	1,539 „
Tea . . . 1,148 „	Chocolate paste .	250 „
Sugar . . . 13,500 „	Preserved milk .	100 pts.
Oatmeal . . . 12 bsh.		
Vinegar . . . 41 gall.	STORES.	
Tobacco . . . ,3,467 lb.		
Soap . . . 2,365 „	Coals	72 ton.
Lime-juice . . 4,136 „	Lignum vitæ . .	3,000 lb.
Scotch barley . 1,280 „	Wood	7 cords.
Rice . . . 300 „	Candles . . .	3,000 lb.
Pickles . . . 4,000 „	Sperm oil . . .	400 gall.
Preserved meats 24,720 „	Linseed . . .	100 „

All stowed in 519 casks, 434 cases, jars, bags, etc., and 7608
preserved meat-tins. The tanks held fifty-one tons,—twenty tons
in provisions and thirty-one tons in water. The consumption of
water was one-third of a ton per day.
    The vessels were doubled and trebled at the bows, and in every
way fitted to resist as much as possible the pressure of the ice.
Crow's-nests were also provided, and a boom for the foot of the
foresail as used by the whalers.

The Whale-fish Islands, eight in number, consist
of large masses of gneiss, piled up in wild confusion and sometimes forming valleys, where moss,
saxifrage and dwarf willow spring up, and small
freshwater lakes are formed by the melting of the
snow in summer. On the rocks, cracked in all
directions by the frost, white and red lichens and
the *tripe de roche*, a plant of a bitter taste but with
some nutritious qualities, are occasionally found.

There are about eighty Esquimaux in the Whale-
fish Islands, and a few half-castes governed by a
Danish carpenter, who when the Erebus and Terror were there was consulted by Sir John Franklin
on the state of the ice to the north. He resides
in a wretched timber house on "Kron-Prins," the
largest island,—yet a palace compared with the
miserable Esquimaux habitations which surround
him; here he collects the skins and oil, and delivers
them over to the Danish vessel, which calls once a
year.

The interior of the adjacent continent of Greenland is covered with an enormous glacier, which
fills up the valleys and ravines, and reduces the
whole extent of country, with the exception of a
narrow strip of bleak and rugged rocks on the sea-
coast, to one vast table-land, gloomy, cold, and
uninhabitable.

The coast is composed of huge granitic rocks,
piled up in the wildest confusion, and intersected by
numerous fiords, or deep channels, which are to be

E

traced sometimes for a hundred miles into the interior, and generally terminate in glaciers; the latter forced on by the pressure of the upper ice-fields, fill the fiord, project far into the sea, and when undermined by the surge, break off in huge masses with a noise like thunder, and form those enormous icebergs which render the navigation of Baffin's Bay so perilous and frequently so disastrous.

The rocks are filled with cracks and fissures, in which garnets and quartz are found; but the vegetation is very scanty, being confined to sorrel, saxifrage, a dwarf ranunculus, some mosses and lichens, which serve as food for the reindeer, dwarf willow, and grass in the marshy ground.

The Esquimaux inhabit this dreary sea-coast from Cape Farewell to the northern extremity of Baffin's Bay, and live entirely on the animals they kill by hunting. The Polar bears, which are very numerous and of enormous size,—sometimes eight or nine feet long, with thin snow-like hair, long necks and narrow heads,—are killed by the natives with the assistance of their dogs. In winter, instead of dens or caves, these animals make their homes under the snow, which, according to the Esquimaux, are constructed with pillars like stately buildings*. The reindeer also are numerous in the southern parts of Greenland, where the natives spend much time in hunting them. White hares and foxes also are caught in stone traps, the remains

* Hans Egede, p. 60.

of which are to be found wherever the Esquimaux have encamped, even on the shores of the remote Parry Islands. The dogs are of a wolfish appearance, with sharp erect ears, and tail curled on the back; eight or ten harnessed to a sledge, and dragging five or six of the largest seals, will make fifteen German miles in the day over rough ice.

Of birds, the ptarmigan, sand-pipers, phalaropes, ravens, owls, falcons, and snow-bunting, are found on land; while immense flocks of gulls, terns, and skuas breed on the small islands and in the clefts of the rocks; the eider, long-tailed and king ducks, brent geese, and every description of the Alcoæ and Colymbidæ are numerous.

The Greenland sea abounds in different sorts of animals. The whales have for many years attracted a large fleet of merchant vessels from England and elsewhere; and among the different species, the Narwhal or Sea Unicorn (*Monodon monoceros*) is the most remarkable. This animal, with its long horn projecting from the snout about fifteen feet, attracts great attention when first seen. The seals on the ice-fields and rocks of Greenland are of several kinds, and form the staple food of the Esquimaux. The sea-horse, with his two large tusks growing downward from his upper jaw about eighteen inches, is a most formidable animal. Fierce encounters sometimes take place between this animal and the white bear, when the latter is often killed.

The seals are speared by the Esquimaux, in their

light ka'aks or canoes, with great dexterity. To
the spear is fastened a line of sealskin, six or seven
fathoms long, at the end of which is a bladder to
prevent the seal from diving after he is struck:
it is pointed sometimes with bone, but near the
Danish settlements, where iron can be procured,
that metal is of course preferred. The canoe is
sharp at both ends, and at most two feet broad,
with a round hole in the centre, just large enough
for a man to insert his body. In these the Esquimaux, with a double paddle, fly through the
water with amazing celerity. Besides the ka'ak,
they have a larger boat, the omenak, for their
women, also made of sealskin.

The Esquimaux, though widely scattered among
the rugged granite cliffs of Greenland, are far from
numerous. Their appearance, with coal-black
long coarse hair, broad shoulders, fetid odour, low
foreheads, sunken eyes, flattened noses, stupid expression, and dwarfish stature, is very repulsive.
Their dress consists of a sealskin frock with a hood,
breeches, and boots; no apparent distinction being
observed between the dress of the two sexes, except
that the women tie their hair up in a knot, instead
of letting it hang over their shoulders.

Their winter habitations are low huts built of
stone, about a yard high and with a flat roof. The
floor is four feet below the level of the ground, to
preserve warmth, and the entrance is by a long
narrow passage. Several families live together in

one of these miserable abodes. The fuel for their
lamps consists of seal-oil, and dried moss supplies
the place of cotton wicks, the smell of which when
combined with raw seal's flesh, fish, and fat, is over-
powering.

Sealskin tents, with the hairy side inwards, are
their summer places of residence, and these are
easily moved from place to place, as the inmates
wander in search of subsistence.

The food of the Esquimaux consists almost entirely of seals' flesh and fish, which is usually eaten
raw, but sometimes boiled or dried in the sun.
Their habits are filthy in the extreme; water never
touching their skin except by accident; while they
do not hesitate to eat offal which would disgust a
starving European.

Such are the Esquimaux of Greenland. The extreme cold, and the hardships to which they have
been subjected for many generations, have had so
baneful an effect upon their minds, that the wondrous works of nature in the regions they inhabit
have not sufficed to soften down or imbue them
with any higher feeling than the mere desire to
satisfy their appetites. The bold granite cliffs of
Greenland, the sense of solitude caused by the
profound stillness, the towering icebergs, the sun
at midnight, the wonderful mirages, the deep blue
of the heavens, has apparently no more effect on
them than upon the bear or fox. Indeed the latter
betray far more intelligence than the lords of crea-

tion in this part of the world! With no method
of improving the mind, and no words in their language to express abstract ideas, the stupid and
insensate state of the Esquimaux's mind forms a
striking contrast to the unobscured clear horizon
and the calm beautiful scenery which surround
him.

During the summer the Whale-fish Islands are
frequented by innumerable flocks of the feathered
tribe. The eider and long-tailed ducks, and divers,
are numerous on the lagoons, and were shot in
great numbers; the Alcidæ of all descriptions
lodge in the clefts of the rocks, and myriads of
gulls swarm upon the calm unruffled sea.

For eight days these islands echoed with the
reports of our guns. Parties were abroad in all
directions, and various devices were resorted to
in order to entrap the unwary birds. The most
amusing stratagem perhaps (one at least which
met with the most applause) was that of two experienced old sportsmen, who floated down towards
the birds in a small dingy, covered with a large
white sheet, to give themselves the appearance of
a lump of ice. On another occasion two officers
(Markham and Hamilton) started on a shooting
excursion, with a heavy four-oared gig. It was a
beautifully calm evening, with a sublime view sea-
ward, where the icebergs floated majestically, and
the horizon was adorned with wonderfully fantastic
mirages. After reaching the northernmost island,

which was hidden from the ships by the intervening
rocks, and spending some hours, the one in shooting, the other in missing, various ducks and divers,
they commenced pulling the boat toward the ships
again. No sooner however had they got midway
between two of the islands, than the bright blue
sky became overcast, and the wind and sea rose
rapidly. In vain they pulled the heavy boat with
all their strength against the opposing waves; she
was rapidly drifting out to sea.   As a last hope
an iceberg was caught hold of with the boathook;
but the waves surged and foamed around it to such
a degree that they were forced to cast off, and again
toiled on at the oars, without however gaining any
ground. The last point of the islands was not more
than half a mile distant, but it seemed to recede
as for hours they pulled the boat towards it—insomuch that it was dubbed then and there Cape
Flyaway.

There was now every prospect of being drifted
out into Davis's Straits; but at length, with the
desperate energy of reviving hope, and the wind
at the same time abating, they reached the long
wished-for point, and obtained a little rest; it was
not however until noon the following day that they
reached the Assistance.

The time was passed in these amusements until
the Expedition was again ready for sea.   On the
25th of June we proceeded northward, and passing
Disco and the Danish settlement of Upernavik,

came for the first time in sight of the broad fields
of ice abreast of the Vrow Islands, and made fast
to an iceberg.

We were surrounded by bergs of all sizes, some
grounded, others drifting. On the evening of the
26th I counted ninety-eight, of many different
shapes,—some with pinnacles, others with domes,
towers, hollow arches, etc., and in the still midnight
huge pieces hourly broke off* in all directions,
with a loud and terrific crash; while every now
and then the whole mass would fall over, making
the sea boil around it†.

It was on the 1st of July that we first entered
the ice, towed by the steamers through a narrow
lane of water, bounded on one side by the broad
fields of ice, and on the other by the perpendicular
granite cliffs of Greenland.   On the 2nd we made
fast to an iceberg, with extensive floes of ice to the
northward, and the Vrow Islands to the south and
westward.

One of the Vrow Islands is faced on its south
side by a perpendicular cliff of red granite, two
thousand feet high, and covered with myriads of
looms‡. A crown of snow covered its upper edge,

* This is called " Calving."

† The specific gravity of an iceberg requires that six-sevenths
shall be under water; and consequently when, by the action of the
water, it is much worn away, the whole mass loses its equilibrium
and capsizes.

‡ Loom—the name given by the whalers to the thick-billed
Guillemot,—*Uria Brunnichii*, 'Guillemot à gros bec' of Tem-

from which descended many clear rills, falling, unbroken by any projecting rock, into the sea.   At
the foot of this cliff three of our boats assembled,
and killed 1080 of these birds, enfilading the ledges
on which they sat, and bringing them down six
and eight at a shot.   When dressed by a skilful
hand, such as the steward of our gun-room, they
make the most delicious soup imaginable.   Many
dovekeys*, several ducks, and a small seal, were
also killed on that day.

The following day we proceeded through lanes
of water to the north, accompanied by several whalers and Mr. Penny's brigs.   The former however,
finding Melville Bay so blocked up with ice that
the season would be lost if they pushed onwards,
turned their heads to the south.   For some days
afterwards we were entirely surrounded by ice, with
not a speck of water to be seen.   At length a lane
of water opened, but the ice as suddenly closed,
and we were forced to cut docks to escape being
crushed to pieces.

Sometimes a narrow strip of ice would inter-
vene between us and the sea to the north, when
the steamers were made to charge full speed at

minck.   The beak is black; neck, back, and tail black; belly
white; legs and toes black; length eighteen inches.

* Dovekey—the whalers' name for the Black Guillemot, *Uria
Grylle*, 'Guillemot à miroir blanc' of Temminck.   Smaller than
the former.   The whole of the plumage is black, except a patch
on the wing, which is white; legs red; length about fourteen
inches.

the ice, while at the same time charges of powder*
were exploded, and thus a way was opened for the
advancing squadron.   When the ice partially gave
way, the excitement was excessive, and every vessel
pushed forward amidst the cracking of hawsers,
singing, cheering, and confusion.

Thus were we impeded by the mighty ice, now
tracking along the edge of the floes, or pressing
into narrow lanes of water, sometimes stopped altogether and nipped by two fields of ice,—playing
rounders, chasing bears, shooting thousands of
rotches†,—with lovely weather, continual daylight,
and strange fairy-like scenery.   On August 14th we
reached the open water off Cape York, in company

* Holes were bored at different places in the ice, and charges
of powder sunk beneath it,—from 2 to 5 lbs., according to the
thickness of the ice. The ice was usually five feet thick ; 2 lb.
charges were exploded two feet and a-half beneath it, and the ice
cracked all round for several yards ; the pieces thus detached were
easily removed. A 5 lb. charge was once exploded nine feet from
the stern of the Assistance, and gave her such a violent shock as
to make all the bells ring. Great caution is therefore necessary.

The blasting charges were contained in glass bottles, earthen-
ware jars, or preserved meat tins. The cork or bung, through
which the fuse is inserted, was rendered water-tight by luting, (a
composition of beeswax and tallow,) and the fuse cut to twelve
inches in length. The charge was made fast to a line, and
lowered down to the required depth ; the hole was then well
tamped down with heavy ice. The fuse burned two feet in a
minute.

† Rotche is the whaler's name for the Little Auk (*Mergulus
melanoleucos*). It is rarely seen on land, except in the breeding
season. They live on small molluscs and crustacea. Captain Parry
shot one in 81° north, (the most northern bird ever seen.) They

with Mr. Penny's brigs, Sir J. Ross's schooner
Felix, and a little vessel commanded by Captain
Forsyth, R.N., destined for Regent's Inlet.

The clearness of the deep blue sky, and the wide
expanse of dazzling ice, bounded by the lofty peaked
mountains and glaciers of Greenland, rendered the
scenery of Baffin's Bay beautiful in the extreme;
but what adds more than anything to the picturesque and almost fairylike appearance of the prospect, are the extraordinary contortions of the land
and icebergs caused by refraction.

Sometimes an iceberg is raised up into the shape
of a lofty pillar, at another a whole chain of them
will assume the appearance of an enormous bridge
or aqueduct, and as quickly change into a succession of beautiful temples or cathedrals of dazzling
whiteness, metamorphosed by the fantastic wand
of nature. Ships too would in appearance rise up
and stand on their heads, with the main trucks of
the real and imaginary one touching. The grandeur of the scenery was rendered tenfold more
beautiful and strange by these wonderful effects,
and during the hard work of pressing through the
ice, our weariness was relieved by beholding this
magnificent panorama, constantly changing and

frequent channels of water separating fields of ice, in Baffin's Bay,
in great numbers, and are excellent in soup. The plumage is
black, except on the belly, where it is white; beak black; legs
yellowish-brown; length eight inches and a-half; of the wing
from the wrist four inches and a-half.

presenting new and more beautiful shapes, like the varying configurations of a kaleidoscope.

Our passage from the Vrow Islands to Cape York, through Melville Bay, took forty-five days; and such were the detentions caused by the ice, that off Cape Walker we were nineteen days making a single mile. The North Star was still more unlucky, being kept sixty-two days in Melville Bay!

Off Cape York we saw several men on the ice, and landing, found them to be the Arctic Highlanders of Sir John Ross. We took one, named Kalahierua, on board, and a story elicited from him about some ships in Wolstenholme Sound detained us to examine into its truth*; while the Resolute proceeded to search Pond's Bay.

It was found that the North Star had wintered here, and the graves of four men, with the date of July 3rd, 1850, showed that she had been but recently liberated from her winter prison. But an appalling spectacle was discovered at a short distance. On the shores of Wolstenholme Sound were several huts, in one of which, huddled together in numbers, lay a heap of human beings. Covered with a sealskin, it was at first uncertain whether they were not our own countrymen; but on its removal, the long black hair, copper-coloured skin,

---

* This was the origin of that fiction about two vessels invented by Adam Beck, Sir John Ross's interpreter, a Danish Esquimaux, who proved to be an outrageous scoundrel.

and high cheekbone, showed them to be the remains of some unfortunate Arctic Highlanders, victims of a recent epidemic.

It was resolved to retain Kalahierua on board, who was named Erasmus York; and we then proceeded westward, in tow of the Intrepid.

Crossing the northern part of Baffin's Bay, we saw the sun set at midnight for the first time since June, in a beautiful calm sea covered with large masses of floating ice which sparkled like diamonds under its rays. On the 18th of August we entered Lancaster Sound, and passed into an uninhabited region where we were destined to spend twelve months without communication with our fellow-men.

After passing Cape Warrender, Captain Ommanney and I landed at the entrance of a harbour never observed before. The ground was covered with mosses, dwarf willow, and saxifrage, growing in comparative abundance. Here also were the remains of several Esquimaux huts, long deserted and strewn with the bones of animals; and about two hundred yards further on I found twelve tombs built of limestone slabs, each containing the skeleton of a native; in one was a skull, with a violent fracture on the left parietal bone.

While we were ashore it came on to blow very hard; the Arctic terns* screamed, whirling in circles round our heads, the waves covered with

* The Arctic tern (*Sterna arctica*), 'Hirondelle de mer Arc-

large masses of ice surged and foamed among the
rocks near the beach, which, added to the violence
of the gale, gave us but faint hopes of regaining
the ships that night.   This newly-discovered harbour was called Port Dundas.

After encountering a heavy gale of wind, and
being becalmed for several hours off Port Leopold,
we reached Cape Riley, when a boat's crew was sent
on shore to erect a cairn; and at this point the first
traces of Sir John Franklin were found.   Pieces of
rope, preserved meat tins, and other remains were
strewn upon the beach*, while higher up the cliff
was a cairn of stones, and a few charges of shot
scattered about.   All this created the greatest excitement, and conjecture was rife whence these remains had come; but at length the discovery of
the name "Goldner" marked upon the meat-tins—
the contractor who had supplied Sir John Franklin
with provisions,—proved to a certainty that a party
from the Erebus and Terror had been at Cape
Riley.

A lead of water however opening up Wellington

tique' of Temminck, has the bill coral red; forehead, crown, and
nape black; wings pearl-grey; tail white; legs orange-red; breast
grey. Length fifteen inches and a-half; wing eleven inches. They
are almost always on the wing. It whirls in circles in the air,
and suddenly darts down with great rapidity on its prey, small
fish.

* Here also was found a long staff, with a cross piece attached
to it. On the cross piece were lashed four bits of iron hoop, bent
like hooks. For what this could have been used no one has
been able to conjecture.

Channel, we pressed forwards, leaving to Captain Austin, Sir J. Ross, the American Expedition, (so generously fitted out by Mr. Grinnell,) and Mr. Penny, the interesting task of searching the adjacent Beechey Island. Their respective vessels shortly afterwards arrived on the spot, and their joint discoveries were deeply interesting. On Cape Spencer Mr. Penny found a carefully paved floor of a tent, and bones of birds in large quantities; sledge tracks also were traced by the Americans one day's journey beyond Cape Innes, where a bottle was found. A large pile of tin canisters was also found on the north point of Beechey Island, and near it was a small oval space, enclosed by a neatly formed border of moss: further on was the foundation of a workshop. But by far the most interesting vestiges of the lost Expedition were three graves, with neatly carved oaken head-boards, and the following epitaphs:—

| Sacred to the Memory of JOHN HARTNELL, A.B. of H.M.S. Erebus, Died Jan. 4, 1846, Aged 25 years. Haggai, c. i. v. 1. "Thus saith the Lord of Hosts, Consider your ways." | Sacred to the Memory of W. BRAINE, R.M., H.M.S. Erebus, Died April 3, 1846, Aged 32 years. "Choose you this day whom you will serve."—Joshua, c. xxiv. v. 15. | Sacred to the Memory of JOHN TORRINGTON, who departed this life January 1st, A.D. 1846, On board of H.M.S. Terror, Aged 20 years. |

Such were the winter-quarters of Sir John

Franklin in 1845–6. No record or document was
found to denote in what direction he had gone;
there stood the graves, and the recent vestiges of
his crews having laboured on those very spots where
the workshops and observatories were found; but
they were gone, nor was there anything to tell the
anxious searcher whither they had sailed. It was
with feelings of mortification and regret that, in
the beginning of September, the vessels left Beechey
Island to continue the search.

Meanwhile the Assistance had been hemmed in
by the ice in the centre of Wellington Channel, and
was in such imminent danger of being crushed to
pieces, that every preparation was made for desert-
ing her. Each person on board was appointed to
a particular boat *; provisions were got on deck,
and every two men were allowed one bag between
them for spare clothes, attached to lines which were
passed through the upper deck, ready to be pulled
up at any moment. One day the vessel was raised
six feet out of water by the pressure of the ice, and
it became so probable that she would fall over on
her broadside, that the men were employed with

---

* The boats of the Assistance were—

1 Life boat . 30 feet long, nine feet broad, (built by White, of
                             Cowes.)
1 Whale boat, 25 ,, ,,   (mahogany.)
1 Cutter   .   23 ,, ,,
4 Ice boats . 25 ,, ,,   (elm, six oars, single bank.)
1 Dingey   .   12 ,, ,,
1 Punt . .   7 ,, ,,

shovels and pickaxes in smoothing a place on the ice for her to lie upon.

Several bears were seen during this time prowling about in search of seals. On one occasion I saw a bear swimming across a lane of water, and pushing a large piece of ice before him. Landing on the floe, he advanced stealthily toward a couple of seals, which were basking in the sun at some little distance, still holding the ice in front to hide his black muzzle; but this most sagacious of bears was for once outwitted, for the seals dived into a pool of water before he could get within reach. On another occasion a female Bruin having been shot from the deck of the Intrepid, her affectionate cub (an animal about the size of a large Newfoundland dog) remained resolutely by the side of its mother, and on the approach of the commander of the Intrepid with part of his crew, a sort of tournament ensued, in which the youthful bear, although belaboured most savagely, showed a gallant resistance, and at length rushing between the legs of the Corporal of Marines laid him prostrate on the ice, floored another man who had seized hold of his tail, and effected his escape.

At length we were enabled to get clear of the ice in Wellington Channel, and passing Cape Hotham were again hemmed in by our remorseless enemy. On September 6th, at 9 a.m., a large floe came down upon us with great violence, and pressing the vessel against the land ice, lifted her several feet

out of the water, and threatened almost instant
destruction. Every one on board rushed on deck
at the first shock, with the exception of the carpenter, a brave and useful man, who coolly sounded
the well to ascertain the depth of water in the hold.
For some hours the ship was in great danger of
being driven on shore; the ice continued to grind
and pile up around her, while all the ice anchors
were laid out, one of which was wrenched in two by
the tremendous strain, and thrown high up into
the air. The wind however providentially changed,
the ice slacked, and we were safe. The land we had
now entered upon was entirely new. Parry indeed
had sighted it, but no human being was ever before
known to have landed on any part of the coast between Cape Riley and Byam Martin Island. There
was therefore all the novelty of a new discovery, as
we coasted along the southern shores of Cornwallis
Island, and came upon a fine bay, which was named
Assistance Harbour.

Proceeding to the westward, our progress was
stopped by a solid barrier of ice, reaching from
Griffith Island to Cape Walker; and here we were
joined by the Resolute, Pioneer, the American Expedition*, and Mr. Penny's brigs. The season for

---

* Advance, Lieutenant Dehaven; Rescue, Lieutenant Griffith.
The American vessels, at the approach of the winter, attempted
to return home. On the 13th of September they advanced as
far as Cape Hotham, but were beset at the entrance of Wellington Channel soon afterwards. On the 18th they were drifted

work however was nearly at an end; the cold was becoming intense, and it was soon found necessary to seek for safe winter-quarters. Mr. Penny succeeded in reaching Assistance Harbour, where he wintered with Sir John Ross; and our squadron was secured to a field of ice between Cornwallis and Griffith Islands.

Thus concluded the working season of 1850. We were now destined to pass the winter further west than any vessel since 1819, and there to prepare for those great efforts for the discovery of Sir John Franklin which were developed during the following spring.

up the Channel, north of Cape Bowden. They drifted slowly to the N.N.W. until the 22nd, when they observed a small island separated from Cornwallis by a channel about three miles wide (Murdagh Isle). To a channel leading north-west was given the name of Maury Channel. The island (called by Penny, Baillie Hamilton) to the N.N.W. was named Grinell Land. On October 20th the vessels were housed over and prepared for winter. During October and November they were drifted about in Wellington Channel. On December 1st they were off Gascoigne Inlet in Barrow's Strait. They continued to drift about six miles a day, and on New-Year's day, 1851, were off Cape Osborn. Dark sky, intimating open water, was observed to the northward in Baffin's Bay. On January 29th the sun appeared. The scurvy now began to be very prevalent. On the 20th of May they were off Cape Walsingham, and on the 27th they passed south of the Arctic circle. On June 6th the floe in which they were imbedded broke up, and they got into open water; and in September, after remaining for some time on the coast of Greenland, they returned to New York.

CHAPTER V.

ARCTIC WINTER QUARTERS.

THE vicelike grasp of the encroaching ice soon fixed the vessels, and we were surrounded by all the accompaniments of an Arctic winter.

The sea entirely disappeared; nothing but one vast icy plain could be discerned from the highest hills of Griffith Isle; every animal, save the bears and foxes, had migrated to the southward; a death-like stillness, broken only by our voices, pervaded all nature; and the cracking of the ice on the beach at flood-tide, and the extreme cold of the clear piercing air, established the reign of Zero*, heralding to us the advent of a severe Arctic Winter†.

Before the season for hibernation had regularly

---

* In the Arctic Expedition, the thermometer being usually below Zero, that word was personified, and looked upon much in the same light as "Jack Frost" is, in an English winter.

† The Expedition was frozen in, in lat. 74° 34′ north, and long. 95° 20′ west, in a strait between Griffith and Cornwallis Isle. The Assistance was one mile from the former, which is a

set in, however, three parties were despatched to lay out depôts for the spring travellers. One pursued its course eastward, and communicated with Sir John Ross and Mr. Penny in Assistance Bay; while the other two went in a westerly direction, encamping the first night under a point, since called Cape Sheringham. No sooner however had they lain down to rest, than the tide rose, cracked the ice over which their tents were pitched, and drenched the unfortunate inmates with half-frozen water. A wild scene of confusion ensued, and the whole party, disturbed from their refreshing slumbers, fled up the beach by the light of the moon.

These two travelling parties, after experiencing very severe weather, and leaving depôts on Somerville Island and Cape Ross, returned to the ships by October 10th. They were the first attempts that had ever been made at travelling in autumn; for until Lieutenant M'Clintock established a depôt for provisions at a distance of at least thirty-five miles from the ships, in a month when the mean temperature was —3°, no Arctic voyager had ventured to dare the rigours of this season.

During the latter part of autumn the tints in the sky are so magnificent, that it would be difficult to draw any comparison with those which we are accustomed to see in other parts of the world.

barren heap of rocks, about fourteen miles long and seven broad, and eight from Cornwallis Land, which is a much more extensive region.

It seems as if the sun displays his most glorious
brilliancy in these regions, where his rays brighten
the gloomy prospect only for a time, compensating
by the increased grandeur of his presence for the
long night which is to follow.   On one side brilliant shades of violet, green, and purple shone forth;
while on the other, lake, crimson, orange, and yel-
low gave a character of more gorgeous splendour
to the eastern sky.

The Aurora Borealis began also to dart its ever-
changing rays across the heavens.   On the 1st of
December a very complete arch, passing through
the zenith, divided the celestial concave into two
equal parts, of a whitish colour tinged with red;
the stars were seen through it with great brilliancy, assuming for the time the same colour as
the Aurora.   On the 5th also some very bright
coruscations were seen to dart their rays towards
the zenith.   Whenever this phenomenon appeared
unusually intense in any particular quarter, a strong
breeze generally succeeded from the same direction.

The parhelia, or false suns, were also very beautiful.   The four false suns are on a brilliant halo
which surrounds the real sun, the upper false sun
being sometimes bisected by an inverted halo.   The
parhelia were connected by streaks of light tinted
with all the colours of the rainbow, with rich golden
rays shooting up from the sun toward the zenith,
and down toward the horizon.

Paraselenæ, or false moons, were also seen during the winter, consisting of a white halo with false moons at the extremities of the horizontal diameter, sometimes tinged with prismatic hues. Such is the splendour of the celestial phenomena, that the pleasure of beholding them is alone worth a voyage to the Arctic Regions; and not only were we enraptured by the beauty of the tints of the sky, the Aurora, the parhelia, and the paraselenæ, but more brilliant meteors still sometimes excited our admiration. On December 2nd one of these phenomena shot through an arc of about 25° with great velocity, and on bursting, a globe of intensely bright pale green detached itself from a scarlet nucleus.

On November the 4th the sun for the last time peeped above the horizon, and then totally disappeared for ninety-five days; but a brilliant twilight continued to light up our noons for many days afterwards, and even in the depth of winter a dim light was visible towards the south, at twelve o'clock, making the surrounding darkness still more palpable. During the month of November it was sufficiently light to enable us to extend our walks to the beach of Griffith Island, to scale its rugged limestone cliffs, and ascend its snow-filled ravines.

One of the latter, almost opposite the ships, was remarkable for its grandeur. Filled with snow to a depth of seventy or eighty feet, its sides rose per-

pendicularly more than four hundred feet, split in
all directions by the action of the frost, the fissures
being filled with transparent ice of the most perfect
azure, while above these rose walls of frozen snow
covered with icicles, dazzlingly white. At certain
intervals the snow seemed to have poured down the
ravine from the overhanging cliffs, and there remained, a hard, firm, inclined plane at an angle of
45°. I remember on one occasion an officer's slip-
ping from the cliff, and sliding down this frozen
road with fearful rapidity, until at length he reached
the bottom of the ravine; but before he could re-
gain his feet, the snowy bed opened, and he disappeared, thus finding in "the lowest depth a lower
deep." It was ascertained that during the summer
a torrent had hollowed out a course in the bottom
of the ravine, arched over by the snow; his weight
had broken the frozen roof, and he was precipi-
tated unhurt into the bed of the now frozen torrent.

The view from the cliffs of Griffith Island presented a scene of gloomy stiffness. All nature appeared to have lost its usual rounded form, and to
show itself divested of all that makes it fitted for
man's dwelling place, its wooded heights, grassy
plains, wide expanse of waters,—in a harsh and
naked angularity. The very piles of ice upon the
beach, with their sharp peaks and jagged excres-
cences, looked like the skeletons of the rounded
surf, that in more favoured climes would have sup-

plied their place. The ships had all the appearance
of frozen pillars, their yards hung with long icy
stalactites; and the broad ice-field, bounded in one
direction by the horizon, and in the other by the
bleak hills of Cornwallis Land, fantastically re-
fracted, gave an unearthly effect to the scenery.

But the cold and darkness soon restricted our
walks to the vicinity of the ships, where every
preparation was made for winter. In the bottom
of the hold a stove was fitted, from which hot-air
pipes were led round the ship; and these, together
with the galley fire and stoves in the gun-room
and captain's cabin, enabled us to keep the lower
deck at a very comfortable temperature during the
whole winter. The upper deck was covered with
hard snow for a depth of two feet, and was roofed
over with a housing of wagon cloth. The sides
were also surrounded by a wall of snow, and a
broad promenade was smoothed round the ship.
The snow was now so hard that it served the pur-
poses of sculpture admirably: posts were erected at
intervals between the ships, and splendid statues,
white as Pentelical marble, of a bear, Britannia,
etc., were carved by artists who, from the knowledge displayed of anatomy and graceful proportion,
would have earned immortal fame had their crea-
tions been of a less perishable material.

The Arctic habiliments adopted were very extraordinary, and sometimes no less ludicrous. The
usual dress was a fur coat and gauntlets, cloth

cap lined with fur, with long additions to cover
the ears and back of the neck, and grey cloth boots
coming half-way up the legs, with thick cork soles.
High fur helmets, fur caps, beaver-skin helmets,
comforters of all colours and dimensions, and even
masks to preserve the nose from the piercing winds,
were not uncommon; but notwithstanding all these
defences against the severity of the weather, the
extreme cold rendered walking very painful, when
there was the least breath of wind; and frost-bites
on the cheeks, nose, ears, and fingers were frequent. The temperature during the winter months
was as follows :—

	Min.	Max.	Mean.
October	—14°	+17°	—3°
November	—30	+14	—7
December	—39	—4	—22
January	—47	—11	—32
February	—48	—13	—33
March			
April	—30	+30	—7

With these low temperatures, spirits, and below
—39 mercury, are frozen; and, strange as it may
appear, this volatile metal, during one of Captain
Parry's voyages, was actually moulded into bullets,
which were rammed down the barrel of a gun and
fired at a mark.

When the cold was accompanied by gales of
wind, which are not uncommon in these regions, it
was impossible to stir outside the ship, and great
volumes of drifting snow were borne aloft and

whirled along the ice, creating vast mountains around the ships, and sometimes entirely burying the smaller steamers. A curious effect is occasionally produced on the snow by these gales, which we noticed: it has been thus described by Baron Wrangel:—" He was guided in his journey by the wave-like stripes of snow (*sastrugi*) which are formed on the level ice of the sea by any wind of long continuance. The ridges always indicate the quarter from which the prevailing winds blow. The inhabitants of the Tundras of Siberia travel to a settlement several hundred wersts off, with no other guide through these unvaried wastes than the *sastrugi*. They know by experience at what angle they must cross the greater and lesser waves of snow in order to arrive at their destination, and they never fail. It often happens that the true, permanent *sastruga* has been obliterated by another, produced by temporary winds; but the traveller is not deceived thereby; his practised eye detects the change, he carefully removes the recently drifted snow, and corrects his course by the lower *sastruga* and by the angle formed by the two*."

But even amidst these gales and snowdrifts, and the piercing cold of an Arctic winter, all modes of search for our missing countrymen were not abandoned. Small gold-beater's skin balloons were inflated, and sent off with hundreds of slips of paper containing information of our position, attached to

* Wrangel's Siberia and Polar Seas, chap. vii., p. 141.

a small match, with the hope that some might drop near the Erebus and Terror.   For the same purpose foxes were caught in traps, and liberated, after attaching to their necks a cylindrical tin case containing a document with the same information, in hopes of their falling in with some of our missing countrymen and being captured by them.

Left in a state of inactivity, to pass the time as we best could, during the gloomy hours of a long continuous night, many amusements were proposed. Guy Fawkes was burnt on the 5th of November, with a display of rockets and blue-lights; a saloon was opened on board the Intrepid, for singing, feats of strength, and other diversions, and two newspapers were published monthly, with the titles of the *"Aurora Borealis"* and the *"Illustrated Arctic News*."*   A theatre was erected on board the Assistance, on a scale of magnificence which, considering the small means at the disposal of the Expedition, was truly marvellous.   In spite of all the difficulties the manager had to encounter, the brilliant and artistic scenery of the "Royal Arctic Theatre" was displayed, to the admiration and delight of the whole Expedition, for the first time on the 9th of November.   The stage was erected on the upper deck, and the front was made of painted canvas.   Doric columns with vases of fruit and

* They have both since been published in England; the former by Colburn, under the title of "Arctic Miscellanies," and the latter by Ackermann and Co.

flowers were painted on each side of the curtain, and two snow statues of the Prince of Wales and the Princess Royal, were placed on either side of the orchestra. The first two nights were confined to farces and songs; but on the 9th of January the famous extravaganza of "Bombastes Furioso" was brought on the boards with great applause; and on February 28th, the last night of the season, the historical drama of "Charles the Twelfth," and a *pantomime* written expressly for the occasion, were brought forward, which produced the greatest mirth and amusement. The pantomime was entitled "Zero, or Harlequin Light;" turning all the dangers and inconveniences to which we were exposed in those inhospitable climes, into evil spirits that were leagued against us. It supposes them continually watching every opportunity to surprise an unfortunate travelling party, till at length their power is destroyed by the appearance of the more puissant good spirits Sun and Daylight. Then the metamorphose takes place. The good spirit Daylight turns into Harlequin; Columbine jumps through an oil-skin sun, which had risen behind the back scene; and frosty old Zero, who has all along been the leader of the evil spirits, is turned into first Clown; a bear, which had been for some time prowling about, was then fired at, and out tumbled Pantaloon and second Clown. Then commenced the pantomime of fun and frolic, which kept the whole party in a roar of laughter from beginning to end.

On board the Resolute, Captain Austin was not unmindful of the experience of a previous voyage, and in the form of a masked ball put into execution a device which he had learned under the able tuition of Captain Hoppner, when first lieutenant of the Fury. A *bal masqué* was accordingly announced on board the Resolute. Captain Ommanney arrived in a splendid sedan-chair, mounted on a sledge, drawn by eight men and attended by a goodly company, as Mayor of Griffith Island. Captain Austin was alternately a " chair-mender," a Carmelite, and a blacking-bottle. The lower deck of the Resolute was crowded with Arabs and Highlanders, old farmers and knights-errant, Jews and jockeys, old women and youthful damsels. The band played lustily until midnight; and the delights of that jovial evening were varied by punch and polkas, whisky and waltzes, cake and quadrilles. It was not until an early hour that the revellers returned to their respective ships, but not without creating considerable amusement to the more sober and steady of the party: the High Priest of Japan, tumbling against a snowy post, measured his length on the frozen sea; Bumble the Beadle was lost in a snowdrift; and the Moorish Chief positively refused to go home until daylight should appear,—a determination which, if persevered in, would in all probability have necessitated his staying out some weeks, if not months.

Such were the sort of amusements which were considered absolutely necessary, and a part of every individual's duty to promote, to drive away the *ennui* that might otherwise have seriously injured both the bodily and mental health of the Expedition. Schools were also established on board each ship, in which the seamen learned reading, writing, arithmetic, trigonometry, and navigation; and the First Lieutenant of the Resolute interested his ship's company by giving lectures on former Arctic voyages. On the 26th of February, when the sun, which had been absent for ninety-six days, again appeared, a party went over to Assistance Bay, and returned with some of Mr. Penny's officers, who were present at our last theatrical exhibition. They had attempted a higher flight, and, without the means which we possessed, had produced one of Sheridan's five-act comedies. All the crews were in good health, and old Sir John Ross sent over two articles for insertion in our newspaper.

But the time of our remaining in winter-quarters was at length drawing to a close. As the month of April approached, preparations were made for the equipment of the travelling parties. The histories of all previous voyages were carefully examined; the greatest attention was paid to the weight of each article to be placed on the sledges; the routes,

time of absence, and depôts for each party, were
all arranged with that minute attention to details
so absolutely necessary in Arctic travelling; and
the officer of every party had to lead his men a
daily walk during the month of March, in order
to train them to fatigue after the long confinement
and inaction of the winter.

Thus carefully were those comprehensive plans
conceived and arranged, which in their execution
have met with such signal success.   In the search
for Sir John Franklin and our missing countrymen, Captain Austin's Expedition may justly lay
claim to having explored and discovered vast tracts
of land hitherto unknown, and done all within the
power of man to effect—even to the loss of limb
and life—in furtherance of the great and humane
cause in which it was embarked.

CHAPTER VI.

ARCTIC TRAVELLING.

THE preparations for an overland search after our missing countrymen were carried on with unceasing energy during the whole of the month of March. Long walks, by way of training, were insisted upon, and as each travelling party had a flag, name, and motto, scattered bodies of men might have been seen, clothed in white duck over their warmer clothing to keep off the drift, and with banners displayed, winding their way up the frowning ravines, crossing the bleak and snow-clad hills, or advancing along the beach of Griffith Isle. Here was the Maltese cross, and the arm transfixing a bleeding heart; there the severed tree; in another direction, the Cornish arms; and again, the red cross of St. George, with many others, waving in the breeze; while those who marched under these several colours exercised their powers of endurance previous to starting on their sacred mission.

G

It was determined that the travelling parties should leave the ships in the middle of April, but a much earlier party was to be despatched to examine the depôts of provisions laid out in the autumn, and I was appointed to it, in company with another officer and seven men. The provisions were stowed on a sledge, together with a tent for sleeping in, and other necessaries*.

The parties left the ships on the 4th of April, more than a month earlier than any travelling party from any of the former expeditions, and when the thermometer was almost constantly below zero. After dragging the sledge over much uneven ice, we arrived at the north-west point of Griffith Island, and pitched our tent for the night. The allowance of provisions for each person per day was as follows :—biscuit, 1 lb. ; boiled pork, 6 oz. ; pemmican, 1 lb. ; rum, 1 gill ; lemon-juice, ¼ oz. ; chocolate, 1½ oz. ; tea, ¼ oz. ; sugar for chocolate, ¼ oz. ; sugar for tea, ½ oz.

The shivering inmates of the tent received their

---

* The sledges were made of American elm, and cross bars of cowdy-wood. The cross bars were lashed on with strips of hide, whilst warm and wet, so that cold would shrink them and keep all tight. The width of each bearer being 2½ inches gave sufficient support by the lashings only, without any stays. If lashed in the cold, the runners would give out at the bottom. The dimensions of the tent were about six feet in perpendicular height, six feet in breadth, and eight feet six inches long ; the breadth however was greatly reduced on the ice by the bagging of the sides, so that it was really not more than five feet or five feet two inches. The sides of the tent were about eight feet four inches.

allowance of a pound of pemmican, boiled in a cooking apparatus by means of a tallow fire, and a gill of rum. After this repast they took off their boots, wrapped their benumbed feet in blanket mocassins, and shook themselves (full dressed with the exception of external shirt and boots) into bags made of blanket, about seven feet long, and thus protected against the cold, disposed themselves to sleep. Thus passed the first night on the frozen sea, and on the following morning the real miseries of Arctic travelling commenced. After drinking a hot pannikin of chocolate, the frightful agony of forcing the feet into boots frozen hard as iron was to be undergone, while the breath, which had condensed on the roof of the tent, fell in thick showers over its half-frozen inmates*. These were some of the miseries which we endured on first rising from bed; but at length, everything being packed up and the men harnessed to the sledge, we were again on foot, bending our steps towards Somerville Island, where, it will be remembered, a depôt had been placed during the previous autumn. On our arrival we found that the tin cases in which the provisions had been packed were torn to ribands, and their contents devoured by the bears, whose wonderful strength had even crushed the solid tin packets of frozen pemmican. Two of these animals approached us on the following day,

* This nuisance might, I think, be obviated by having ventilating holes at certain intervals in the upper part of the tent.

and, after a long chase, the female was killed and
converted into fuel.

Our luncheon consisted of a piece of pork fat,
frozen so hard that it broke like biscuit, and half
a gill of rum, to drink which out of a tin pannikin required considerable caution and experience,
to prevent the cold metal from taking the skin off
the imbiber's lips. How applicable are the lines
of Hudibras in these regions !—

> "Ah me! what perils do environ
> The man that meddles with cold iron."

Luncheon indeed was but a sorry meal : we
merely stopped in the middle of the march for one
quarter of an hour, to eat our pork fat and to
drink our allotted dram of spirits,—a proceeding
which was usually accomplished while running up
and down on the ice, to keep up the circulation
and escape being frost-bitten. The glare of the
snow during the march frequently caused *snow-
blindness,* a species of ophthalmia of a most painful
kind.

On the 11th of April, Mr. M'Dougall having
made his report, we again started, at 8 A.M., to
examine and replenish the autumn depôt on Cornwallis Island, and explore Brown Island and the
coast to the westward of the depôt. We were
dragged for some miles by the other travelling
parties, who gave us three cheers on parting, and
at 3.30 P.M. we arrived on the south-west point of

Cornwallis Island, which we named Cape Endeavour, after our sledge, and an island in the bay
beyond we called Marryatt Island.

The next day, (according to my journal, from
which I am now giving some literal extracts,) we
started across the bay towards the next point, par-
took of luncheon a little south-by-west of Marryatt
Island, and got a lat. 74° 45′ north. At half-past
four we reached a long low point, which we named
Point Frazer, the bay being about ten miles across,
and deep, surrounded by hills. We had a beautiful
view of the bay beyond, in which is an extensive
and deep inlet, also noticed by Mr. M'Clintock in
the autumn.

April 13, *Sunday.*—Blowing fresh. I walked
over Frazer Point, where there is a ledge of rocks
very full of quartz. 10 A.M. Started with a fair
wind (sail of much use), and at 6 P.M. came to on
the floe, nearly opposite the deep inlet.

During the whole of the next day it was blowing so strong a gale of wind, with the thermometer at +2, that we were confined entirely to the
tent. My solace, under these circumstances, was
a volume of Hudibras. Passed a good night.

April 15.—Very foggy, and snowing hard. At
1.15 P.M. arrived on an autumn depôt point, which
was entirely covered with snow. Found three
cases of pemmican, twelve cases of chocolate, and
two potato-cases, torn to pieces by the bears and
quite empty, the same as at Somerville Island.

Employed ourselves for some time in digging a hole, to contain the renewed depôt, which we completely finished by 6.30 P.M. I took a walk over the hills, but there was too much mist for me to get any view of the surrounding country. Supper, and turned in.

April 16.—Thick misty day. Found, to our utter discomfiture, that the spirit-lamp was left behind at our last resting-place, and were employed during the whole of the forenoon in making one from a *bouilli* tin. This was absolutely necessary, as spirits-of-wine or the fat of bears, when we could kill them, was our only fuel either for procuring warmth or cooking. I took a walk along the beach, and found a long shallow lagoon between the first and second ridges of limestone shingle. This is the most desolate-looking part of Cornwallis Island that I have yet seen: covered with snow, with hardly a rock or large stone to relieve the eye, the broad plain stretches away and bounds the view on the tops of the hills; while, round the beach, the thick clouds hanging heavily over the floe, or ever and anon sweeping fitfully along the great hummocks of ice that are piled upon the shore, present a scene of unequalled wretchedness and desolation. A concert took place before supper. 7 P.M. On looking out of the tent, the only thing visible was a staff with my pocket-handkerchief flying from it, the mist obscuring everything else. Singing till midnight.

April 17.—Started at 8.30; skirting along the
low land to the northward.   The fog suddenly
cleared off, and we discovered land stretching round
us, and forming a deep bay.   At 1.30 P.M. landed
on a low shingly beach.   I picked up a fossil bi-
valve and some corallines.   Land very low, with
hills inland.   3 P.M. Reached the end of the bay,
and landed on the same kind of beach, the bay
being about six miles deep.   5 P.M. Reached a
long point, which we supposed to be part of
Bathurst Island, and encamped there.   Walked
over the top of the point, where I found much
moss and hare-dung.   The tent was delightfully
comfortable, owing, no doubt, to its crowded state,
two of our company being obliged to lie upon the
rest, and thus producing considerable warmth; my
berth was always against the canvas at the furthest
end from the door.

April 18.—Blowing fresh with much drift: we
were consequently confined to the tent, which is
pitched on the beach just inside a pile of hummocks
of ice; from the door the hill gradually rises to
a height of about one hundred feet, where the
table-land on the point commences, being about
a mile and a half long and half a mile broad.
This evening we began to use the spirits-of-wine,
and it took two gills and a half to boil a kettle
for soup, and half a gill for water for grog—a
process which, it must always be remembered,
was performed in the same kettle.

April 19.—We remained at this point to obtain a latitude, so I took the opportunity of wandering over the table-land till noon. But the sun being obscured, we started for the next autumn depôt point after luncheon, and, having seen a snow-bunting on the way, arrived there at 5.30 P.M., when we found that the north-west division had left it on the night of the 18th, all well. Pitched the tent and had supper.

April 20.—Made our tea for breakfast by burning moss, and used no spirits-of-wine. At 9 A.M. started for Brown Island; very misty. After luncheon I went ahead, and landed on the north-east point of Brown Island, and walked all over it, returning to the tent, which was pitched on the north-east point. The south-west part of the island consists of perpendicular limestone cliffs, rising to a height of about 450 feet; the top forms a valley, where the inner faces of the cliff slope gradually inland, producing various hollows, in which are small lagoons and some moss. The north-east part of the island is formed by the *débris* which has been washed down from the high land, and consists of limestone shingle, sloping very gradually in terraces, and ending in a long low point, on which we were encamped. It came on to blow a heavy gale of wind. A very cold night. Thermometer −3.

April 21.—Remained here during the day, to obtain a latitude, which we found to be 71° 49′ 10″

north. In the afternoon M'Dougall got a round
of angles. 6 p.m. Supper, and turned in.

April 22.—A bitterly cold morning, thermometer at 8 a.m. −17. Started at 9.30 for the
ships, over a good floe for travelling. At 12, Capes
Martyr and Endeavour appeared before us in a line;
land opening gradually. A very cold wind blowing, with thermometer −20; most trying to the
ears, nose, and fingers. At 6.p.m. pitched tent on
the floe for the night. Supper, and turned in.
Though the thermometer showed fifty-two degrees
of frost, we did not suffer so much from the cold as
on the previous night.

April 23.—Started for the ships; during the
early part of the forenoon the floe was very hum-
mocky. At 10, came in sight of the ships. Had
luncheon off the north-west point of Griffith Island,
and, with a fair wind, the sledge arrived alongside
the Resolute by 1.30 p.m.

We had been altogether nineteen days travelling; and though the thermometer was at one time
as low as −30, blowing fresh, yet neither I nor
any one else of the party suffered in any great
degree from frostbites; and after a hard day's
work we enjoyed no small comfort in our blanket
bags, two of which were allowed to us, as we had
but one wolf-skin. All the men wore carpet
boots, with blanket wrappers and stockings (their
feet being examined every night by one of the
officers), instead of the canvas boots worn by the

other parties, which accounts for their not being frost-bitten, as the canvas boots are tight across the toes, and will not admit of free circulation. For several days we were confined to the tent by the violence of the gales, but during the nineteen days we had travelled 140 miles. This journey may be taken as a type of those which followed during the remainder of the season. Meanwhile the other parties, which were destined for more extensive search, and to be absent a much longer period, had assembled in two great divisions, under the respective commands of Captain Ommanney and Lieutenant M'Clintock, previous to leaving the ships under the north-west bluffs of Griffith Island. Here they were closely examined, to see that they were provided with everything that could contribute to the success of the great undertaking they had in hand; and, with a view to encourage them in their arduous task, and to instil into the men the spirit and enthusiasm which such a course demanded, and the privations they would be exposed to would inevitably call for, Captain Austin, who was to remain with the ships, addressed them in a short but emphatic speech on the 15th of April. "As the one entrusted with the Expedition," he said, "it has been a cause of sincere satisfaction to me to behold the unanimity and good feeling towards each other that has existed throughout our little community from the day we embarked under one head, and for one cause; and

I may add, that from the time these extensive operations, entailing labour and privation, have been made known, the high spirit and real earnestness with which all have entered into the preparation has afforded me the highest gratification, and enables me to look forward with much confidence to the future. In conclusion, I beg to assure all present that, although I shall not be personally sharing the toil with them, yet my anxious, warmest wishes and earnest prayers will be in constant action for their protection and guidance until their return."

It was a cold murky day, that 15th of April, with the wind drifting the snow in fitful gusts around the hummocks of ice that were piled upon the beach. The divisions separated at once, Captain Ommanney's proceeding toward Cape Walker, and Lieutenant M'Clintock's westward in the direction of Melville Island.

We will, in the first place, follow Captain Ommanney. On the very first day the strength of the wind, and the weight of the sledges, together with the uneven hard ridges of snow, rendered the work of dragging very laborious. During the night the travellers heard the ice crack and groan under their tents. As they approached Cape Walker the scene around was one of peculiar solitude and gloom, —nothing but a snowy desert, without a speck for the eye to rest on. " Human life seemed obtrusive and unwelcome in such a scene of desolation."

On the 21st the party arrived at Cape Walker, an abrupt and lofty headland; but a line of ice hummocks intervened between the sledges and the beach, which was not to be crossed except by un-loading and double-manning them. Here a furious gale of wind confined every one to the tents; the gusts off the high land moaned and rattled round the canvas houses almost incessantly, and even blew through them, creating frostbites on the noses and fingers of the men while asleep in their blanket bags.

At this point Lieutenant Brown proceeded south, and discovered a considerable tract of previously unknown coast, and returned to the ships, having been absent forty-five days.

Captain Ommanney and the other parties ad-vanced to the south-west along a low unknown coast of limestone formation, until, on the 30th, they reached a deep inlet, which was discovered by Lieutenant Mecham to form a strait, dividing the large island of Russell—one hundred miles in cir-cumference—from Prince of Wales's Land. Be-yond the northern outlet of this channel the land extends west-south-west for twenty-five miles of low dreary coast, covered with snow, where a deep gulf, fifty miles in circumference, was explored, which has since been called after Captain Ommanney, while Lieutenant Osborn searched some distance to the southward. They had now come to the extreme limit of their journey without meeting a vestige of any European having ever set foot on those shores. From the shoalness of the water at considerable distances from the shore, and the great thickness and apparent age of the ice, it is probable that these seas are seldom, if ever, navigable for ships. Great had been the mortification of the travellers when no sign of Sir John Franklin's expedition had been discovered on Cape Walker, where it had been generally supposed that traces would have been found if he had proceeded in that direction: and now three hundred miles of land had been discovered and thoroughly examined, without a trace of the missing ships,—all that was seen was a barren coast, covered with snow and bounded by the frozen sea,—monotonous, dreary, and inhospitable.

On the 6th of June Captain Ommanney commenced his return homewards, and on the 12th, the day before he arrived at the ships, the party met with a laughable accident, although it might have had a serious termination. They had all of them but just got into their blanket bags, when a peculiar noise, as if something was rubbing up the snow, was heard outside. The gallant Captain instantly divined its cause, seized, loaded, and cocked his gun, and ordered the tent-door to be opened, upon which a huge bear was seen outside. Captain Ommanney fired at the animal, but, whether from the benumbed state of his limbs, or the dim glimmering light, he unfortunately missed him, and

shot away the rope that supported the tent instead.
The enraged monster then poked its head against
the poles, and the tent fell upon its terrified inmates, and embraced them in its folds. Their confusion and dismay can more easily be imagined
than described, but at length one man, with more
self-possession than the rest, slipped out of his bag,
scrambled from under the prostrate tent, and ran
to the sledge for another gun : and it was well that
he did so, for no sooner had he vacated his sleeping sack than Bruin seized it between his teeth
and shook it violently, with the evident intention
of wreaking his vengeance on its inmate. He was
however speedily despatched by a well-aimed shot
from the man, the tent was re-pitched, and tran-
quillity restored.

After an absence of sixty days Captain Ommanney arrived on board the Assistance; Lieutenant Osborn, who had accompanied him, returned the pre-
ceding day. The former thus concludes his report :
" It is a consolation to know we have thoroughly
examined all the coast within our reach, and personally explored two hundred geographical miles
of newly discovered land. Although unsuccessful
in meeting with traces, my mind is firmly convinced
of the impracticability of any ships navigating along
this coast, for these reasons—shoals extend along
the great part of it, and I could see no indication
of currents or tide-marks, and, from the nature
of the ice, it is impossible to say what time the

oldest of it may have taken to accumulate, probably for many seasons; consequently I entertain
no hopes of ships ever reaching the continent of
America south-west of Cape Walker."

Meanwhile the division under Lieutenant M'Clintock had proceeded rapidly to the westward along
the southern shores of Cornwallis and Bathurst
Lands: the cold was so intense that several men
received frostbites on the toes, and were obliged to
be sent back with the returning sledges to the ships.
In one of these cases the mortification was so rapid
that death ensued twenty-four hours after the suf-
ferer had arrived on board*. " It was with sincere
regret," says Lieutenant M'Clintock, "that I bade
farewell to those poor fellows, whom it had become
necessary to send back. Unconscious of the danger
of neglecting the extremities, and despising the
pain which labour occasioned, they still desired to
go on, and their sad countenances betrayed the
bitter disappointment felt at being unable to proceed further on our humane mission." On the 1st
of May the parties of M'Clintock and Bradford
arrived on Byam Martin Island, where they separated; the former pressed on to the westward, and
the latter, having discovered the east coast of Melville Island as far north as 76° 15′, returned to the
ships after an absence of eighty days. Lieutenant
Aldrich also discovered the west coast of Bathurst

* Besides this death from frostbite, four men suffered ampu-
tation of their great toes, and one of part of his foot.

Land up to 76° 11', and returned after an absence of sixty-two days.

On the 10th of May Lieutenant M'Clintock landed on the south-east point of Melville Island, being the first human being who had visited that distant land—the Ultima Thule of modern times— since 1820. He was now, with his six men, thrown entirely on his own resources, exposed to all the vicissitudes of a rigorous climate, and dependent on his own efforts, and the accidental condition of the ice, for advance or retreat.

While the sledge skirted the shores of Melville Island from point to point, with a sail set, which proved of great assistance, Lieutenant M'Clintock carefully examined all the indentations of the coast, and shot several hares and ptarmigan, which were now beginning to make their appearance.

On the 16th they passed through a gigantic range of hummocks of ice, resembling a ruined wall, averaging twenty feet in height, and apparently piled up by enormous pressure; and on the 19th a herd of musk-oxen (*Ovibos moschatus*) were seen grazing near Cape Bounty: two of these animals were killed, but only 8 lbs. of fat and 150 lbs. of beef was obtained from them. A small herd of reindeer were also seen.

Passing the winter harbour of Parry, the land near Cape Providence was found to consist of ranges of hills with a narrow belt of low land, containing many well-sheltered and comparatively fertile spots. Further to the westward the cliffs, 450 feet high, rose directly from the sea, broken occasionally by broad ravines, in one of which there rose up a perpendicular sandstone pinnacle. Along this coast the ice is so rough, that Sir Edward Parry called it "hill and dale,"—as if the ocean waves had suddenly frozen, and become studded with hemispherical mounds of ice.

Rounding Cape Dundas, the extreme point seen by Parry, Lieutenant M'Clintock reached the furthest west ever attained by any European in these regions, which has since been called Cape James Ross*; and ascending a cliff 700 feet high, observed Banks's Land, which appeared to be very lofty, with steep hills and large ravines. A coastline, consisting of a part of Melville Island, was also discovered, seventy-five miles in length, and forming, with Banks's Land, the two coasts of a strait, which at the extreme western points was sixty-six miles in breadth†. This is probably the North-West Passage.

The party had now arrived at a distance of three hundred miles from the ships in a direct line, when

* Lat. 74° 41′ N., Long. 114° 26′ W.

† From the position of Cape James Ross, the angle subtended between the western extreme of Banks's Land, and that of the newly discovered land, was 57°. These extremes appeared distant respectively about twenty leagues and twenty-five leagues, therefore the breadth of the Strait at this point must be sixty-six miles.

it became necessary to commence the return home; and accordingly they proceeded up Liddon's Gulf and on the 1st of June reached Bushnan Cove. Here it was that Sir John Franklin, or some of his crew, if they had wintered anywhere to the north of Melville Island, would have left some traces in an attempt to reach the continent of America; but not a vestige was to be found.

In this picturesque spot Parry had left his travelling cart on the 11th of June, 1820, and Lieutenant M'Clintock found the wheels, which he used for fuel, several tin water-bottles, and even the bones of the ptarmigan Parry had dined off. Thus, after an interval of thirty years, did these explorers revisit the place where the first Arctic travellers had encamped.

Crossing the land from the head of Liddon's Gulf, the party arrived at Winter Harbour on the 5th, and encamped near the mass of sandstone at its entrance, on which the names of the "Hecla" and "Griper" were carved.

The foundations of Parry's observatory were found, with pieces of wood, broken glass, nails, and a domino,—rare things in these desolate regions! Here also they found a hare, which dwelt within twenty yards of their tent, and remained on the most friendly terms with them during the whole of their stay, regarding them with the utmost confidence, and even allowing the men to touch her. There can scarcely be a more convincing proof than this, that our missing countrymen had not been there. On the 8th of June the weather had become so warm, that drink was enjoyed off Cape Bounty without the aid of fire; and from that time the snow began to melt, which occasioned additional discomforts; for the tent and baggage on the sledge frequently got wet and the men had to wade incessantly through water up to their knees, so that the extreme cold and frost-bites of Spring were replaced by the wet and misery of an Arctic Summer. After a long and weary walk of 250 miles, Lieutenant M'Clintock arrived on board on the 4th of July, and thus terminated the most extraordinary journey in the annals of Arctic history. His party had been absent eighty-one days, during which time they had travelled over 770 miles of ground, averaging a distance of ten miles daily.

Such was the crowning effort of the Spring searching parties of Captain Austin's expedition; and Lieutenant M'Clintock thus modestly concludes his journal:—" Although some considerable degree of disappointment is at all times the result of an unsuccessful expedition, the more so when its object is to relieve our fellow-creatures in their utmost extremity, yet in justice to my own feelings, and to those men whose labours have enabled me to fulfil my instructions, I cannot conclude this account of a journey of eighty days without expressing the satisfaction their conduct has afforded me. Their ever cheerful behaviour, untiring perse-

verance, and patient enduring spirit, under many
severe trials and privations, excited my warmest
admiration.   For the blessings of health, strength,
and exemption from accident, without which we
must have sunk under the difficulties of this undertaking, our deepest gratitude is due to "the
Giver of all good gifts."

Another party from Captain Austin's ship discovered the deep bay dividing Cornwallis and Bathurst Lands, and which is terminated on the west
by Markham Point, and on the east by a narrow
inlet; while Mr. Allen, Master of the Resolute, examined the shores of Lowther and Garrett Islands.

Meanwhile the expeditions in Assistance Bay had
not been idle.   Mr. Penny, with considerable zeal
and ability, had prepared two sledge parties, which
examined part of the east and west shores of Wellington Channel; and he himself, in a dog-sledge,
and afterwards in a boat, explored the islands
previously seen by the Americans, and called by
them Grinell Land.   Here some open water, caused
by a strong current, was seen in May, but of what
extent is very doubtful.   How many miles these
parties travelled, and in what exact direction, it is
impossible to say, from the want of observations,
and the distances being greatly overrated.   No
vestige however of Sir John Franklin was found in
the course of Mr. Penny's explorations; so that,
beyond the winter-quarters at Beechey Island, not
a trace had been discovered,—not a clue, by which

to determine his fate, or to guide us in continuing the search*. Sir John Ross also dispatched a party into the interior of Cornwallis Land, but without reaching its northern shores.

Such were the exertions made during the spring of 1851, to discover and relieve our long-lost countrymen. Five parties of Captain Austin's expedition were away from the ships much longer than any that had preceded them, and braving the hardships of a month, the mean temperature of which was −7, and the maximum 39; they have, although unsuccessful in the main object, at least done their utmost, and well merited the praise which has been bestowed upon their gallant and untiring efforts.

---

* A piece of elm, indeed, was found by Mr. Penny on one of the islands in Wellington Channel, lat. 76° 2′ N., eighteen inches long (a fragment of an inch-thick elm board), but it was decided by Sir John Richardson, that from the length of time it takes in these high northern latitudes to decompose and bleach woody fibres to the extent that this process had advanced, and to develope the lichenoid bodies (*perithecia*) found on it, it must have been exposed to the weather at least ten years, and probably much longer, and that therefore it has no connection with Sir J. Franklin's expedition. From its being tarred it must have belonged to civilized men; but it might have drifted up from a whaler in Baffin's Bay, as such things have been known to take place; for instance, a part of an oar was found on Cape Hotham, marked "Friendship,"—a whaler wrecked several years before in Baffin's Bay.

CHAPTER VII.

THE PARRY ISLANDS.

IF we look on the map of the world, to the northward of the great continent of America, a long
line of blue will be seen running east and west from
Baffin's Bay far into the unknown Arctic regions,
and bounded on the west by a wide expanse of
white, which denotes the land or ice as yet undis-
covered.

The northern shores of this sea are divided into
two extensive masses by Austin Channel; the one
consisting of Cornwallis and Bathurst Lands, and
the other of Melville Island. These, with a number of smaller islands, form the Parry group, which
was discovered by Sir Edward Parry in 1819-20,
and first explored by Captain Austin's Expedition
in 1850-51.

This barren country, from Wellington Channel
to Bedford Bay, is composed of limestone, forming
monotonous ranges of hills, broken here and there
by the action of the frost, and by deep ravines;

while Bathurst and Melville Lands, from Bedford Bay to the westernmost point hitherto attained, are composed of sandstone.

To the southward of Barrow's Strait, the two masses of land called North Somerset and Prince of Wales's Land, the one explored by Sir James Ross and the other by Captain Ommanney, are of a different character. North Somerset consists partly of limestone and partly of sandstone, and gypsum has also been found here in considerable quantities; while Prince of Wales's Land, with the exception of Cape Walker, which is formed of sandstone and conglomerate, is entirely composed of limestone.

There are few more interesting studies than that which treats of the state of our planet, the strange monsters which inhabited it, and the convulsions it underwent previously to the creation of man. In the gradual development of organic beings, from the first appearance of the lowest radiated animals till Adam was formed in the image of his Creator, each class of animals seems in its turn to have exercised a paramount authority for a considerable period, until a new order of things ushered into the world still mightier agents with more complicated wants. At length all nature teemed with animal and vegetable life, of every size and form, from the humblest *Infusoria* to the *Bimana,* whose dominion extends over all created beings.

The fossil organic remains, both animal and

vegetable, which are strewn over every continent,
to chronicle the generations of beings that lived
and died ages before the Mosaic creation, have un-
folded this marvellous history of the pre-Adamitic
world. The highest class of fossil animal found in
the Parry Islands was a species of *Crustacea,* which
is widely scattered along the shores of Griffith and
Cornwallis Islands, and is called the Trilobite, from
the hard rings covering its body and dividing it
into three lobes. It was a voracious animal, feeding probably on the molluscs, annelids, and *Acrita;*
but it is now extinct, and may be supposed to be
the type from whence in the course of ages the
more perfect lobster and crab are derived.

In the limestone of the Parry Islands, the *Ce-
phalopoda,* or highest order of Molluscs, are repre-
sented by the *Orthoceras,* a siphuncled shell, like
the Nautilus, uncoiled and straightened, which is
found in great numbers. The only species of uni-
valve in the order *Gasteropoda* which I found, was
one of the *Turritellæ* or spire-shells, tolerably perfect. Several descriptions of fossil bivalves were
collected on different parts of Griffith Island. But
the most beautiful remains of another age were
the Encrinites, which lay in heaps upon the slabs
of limestone: they were a species of radiated
animal, commonly called Stone-lilies, which found
nourishment by moving their bodies through a
limited space from a fixed position at the bottom
of the sea. Corals also of various kinds were nu-

merous, some of them very perfect and forming semi-spheres.

These were the principal fossils found in the limestone of the Parry Islands.

The sandstone of Melville and Byam Martin Islands is evidently of the carboniferous era, from the coal which has been found on several parts of their coasts. Captain Parry collected considerable quantities; and between Capes Dundas and Hopner, and still further to the westward, Lieutenant M'Clintock found much coal, but of such quality that it would not burn alone.

During the winter these regions are covered with hard frozen snow, and all vegetation becomes invisible. The sea spreads forth its broad white surface, unbroken even by the majestic icebergs which are so numerous in Baffin's Bay, but which are never seen near the shores of the Parry Islands. This may be accounted for by the fact, that the small quantity of continuous land, together with the crumbling nature of the limestone, has prevented the formation of glaciers — the mighty parents of the icebergs; while on the more solid granite and gneiss of Greenland, the enormous weight of superincumbent snow is easily supported.

The numerous small lakes formed in all the hollows of land in the Parry Islands are frozen to the bottom, and are perfectly transparent; while the larger ones are deeply frozen over, but contain

small fish (*Salmo aulopus*) which were procured by
Mr. Penny's people in the depth of winter.   In
the sea, the seals are believed to remain without
migrating to the southward, and to retain life by
keeping open holes in the ice, while a sufficiency
of air penetrates through the snow.   Some were
seen on the ice in the middle of April.

Every other living creature leaves this desolate
land, and seeks shelter in warmer climates by the
end of September, except three hardy quadrupeds,
of very different sizes, viz. the Bear (*Ursus ma-
ritimus*), the White Fox (*Canis lagopus*), and the
Lemming (*Arvicola Hudsonica*).   The former of
these animals is supposed never to hibernate, but
to prowl about the whole winter through in a probably fruitless search after seals.   The foxes were
frequently caught in traps, in the coldest months,
usually in good condition, from feeding probably
on the last-mentioned animal, the little Lemming.
This is a small species of *Rodentia*, with burrowing
feet like the mole, which forms its home under the
snow, and lives on the little granary of seeds it has
collected in the summer*.

Such are the only living things that endure
the winter of these inhospitable Arctic islands,
which in that rigorous season are wild and bleak

---

* We had one of these on board for some time, which used to
run about the table at dessert, and eat bits of walnut and biscuit
out of our hands; frequently nestling up our sleeves, or in the
palms of our hands.   It died before our return to England.

indeed. The beach is generally forced up into a succession of shingly terraces by the hummocks of ice which line the shores, while the cliffs are lofty and almost perpendicular, especially in Griffith Island, where they attain an average height of 500 feet.

Thus from September to May these regions are vast solitudes; but then some few animals begin to appear, although the snow still covers the land, and no thaw has taken place. The first that arrives is the White Hare (*Lepus glacialis*), which usually weighs about 10 lbs. and is excellent eating; the Ptarmigan (*Tetrao lagopus*), and the Snow Bunting (*Emberiza nivalis*). All these animals are perfectly white when they first arrive, but gradually change their colour as the summer advances.

When however the month of June is set in, and more genial weather arrives with the returning sun, the face of nature begins to wear a more cheerful aspect. The snow melts on the hills, and running into the hollows, small lakes are formed, which, though covered throughout the summer with large pieces of floating ice, form a striking contrast to the snowy wastes they have replaced.

Some scanty vegetation now begins to show itself on the otherwise naked rocks. Small tufts of moss, sorrel, purple saxifrage, a dwarf ranunculus, and *Stellaria Rossi*, appear in the sheltered spots, while the marshy grounds are covered with grass and moss. On one broad plain on the western shore of Griffith Island was a granite boulder, under shelter of which a tuft of rank moss covered with bones appeared, showing that on this spot an aged bear had lain down to die, and like a true patriot added to the fertility and vegetation of his country. The whole plain indeed was covered with similar patches, and in the centre of each were universally found the bones of bears, foxes, or birds. It appeared to be the great cemetery, and consequently the most fertile plain, of Griffith Island.

The largest plants in the Parry Islands are the dwarf willow, which does not rise more than two inches from the ground, and whose stunted branches creep in lowly insignificance among the surrounding stones; and the club-moss (*Andromeda tetragona*), which however has only been seen at Melville Island, and there in small quantities.

The warm sun of July and August, always above the horizon, brings out swarms of mosquitos, which hover over the lakes; and Lieutenant M'Clintock even mentions having seen caterpillars near Cape Dundas; but it is probable that the cold prevents their ever arriving at the more perfect and beautiful stage of their existence.

The Reindeer migrate northward in May, but few have been met with to the east of Melville Island, where one was shot and thirty-four were seen. A few were also observed on the hills of Bathurst Land, and one of Mr. Penny's parties reports having

seen a herd on the shores of Wellington Channel.
The Musk Oxen are entirely confined to Melville
Island, where Lieutenant M'Clintock shot four,
and saw forty-six.   Beyond Point Hearne he got
within two hundred yards of eight of these animals,
which galloped suddenly away for a few yards,
halted, and formed for defence in a semicircle,
close together, with their heads down, and their
strangely curved horns resembling a row of hooks
in a butcher's shop.   When within a hundred
yards he shot the largest one, but the rest were
not in the least discomposed, and continued in
the same posture, until he retired to a considerable distance, when they renewed their search for
pasture.

As June passes on, great flocks of ducks, gulls,
and guillemots come to breed in the Parry Islands,
where they are comparatively free from the depre-
dations of wolves, only one of which was seen, and
wounded in Liddon's Gulf.

By the beginning of July all the travelling parties
had returned to the ships, and between this time
and our liberation from the ice, shooting parties
were organized to collect on the face of the cliffs,
and the banks of lagoons, some fresh provisions
for the sick.

On the south-east point of Griffith Island is a
perpendicular cliff, 500 feet high, covered with
dovekeys, glaucous gulls, fulmar petrels, and the
ivory gull,—a bird whose plumage is as white as the

driven snow. Under the cliff a prodigious land-
slip of huge blocks of limestone had fallen. Some
stood upright nearly square, and twenty feet in
height; others in the shape of pyramids twenty-
five feet high, and split into perpendicular layers,
with the moss and purple saxifrage growing
thickly in all directions; and thus they blocked
up the beach from the foot of the cliff to the sea.
It was indeed a scene of wild confusion. Standing
near this tremendous convulsion of nature, with
the perpendicular cliff towering overhead, and the
gulls whirling and screaming in the air, how
sublime to have witnessed the fall of these huge
masses of rocks, weighing thousands of tons, and
to have heard the tremendous crash, succeeded by
a profound and deathlike silence!

A shooting party under Lieutenant Cator was
stationed at this point until late in July, supplying
the squadron with guillemots and gulls.

The lagoons of Griffith and Cornwallis Islands
were frequented during the summer by numerous
flocks of eider ducks (*Anas mollissima*), king ducks,
a beautiful bird with tints of purple, green, and
gold about the head (*Somateria spectabilis*), long-
tailed ducks (*Fuligula glacialis*), and brent geese
(*Anser torquatus*), many of which were shot by the
sportsmen of the expedition. The red-throated
diver (*Colymbus septentrionalis*) was sometimes,
though more rarely, seen, probably from its being
a bird of greater cunning. It builds its nest on

some little mossy islet in the centre of a lagoon, secure from the molestations of the fox. On a small low stony island in Allen Bay, surrounded by lofty hummocks of ice, which rendered the land almost invisible from the sea-level, the sole inhabitant was one of these wary birds. Red-necked phalaropes (*Phalaropus hyperboreus*) and curlew sandpipers (*Tringa subarquata*) were also frequenters of these wilds; and the ring dottrel (*Pharadius*) was seen, though seldom. Solitary ravens sometimes flew gloomily along the shore, with their necks encircled by a white band of congealed breath; and noisy little Arctic terns, silver gulls (*Larus argentatus*), skuas (*Lestris parasiticus*), and kittiwakes (*Larus tridactylus*), were among the less common of the winged tribe*.

All these birds leave this desolate region by the end of September, so that the Parry Islands are only enlivened by their presence four months in the year.

Meanwhile, as the blue water once more begins to appear, and break up the vast plain which had so long usurped its place, the inhabitants of the

---

* Birds killed by a shooting party round Griffith Isle; two guns; from June 26th to July 2nd:—Eider ducks, 6; brent geese, 2; fulmar petrels, 3; Arctic tern, 1; phalarope, 1; ptarmigans, 3; dovekeys, 14. Total, 30 birds.

Birds killed by a shooting party on Cornwallis Isle; five guns; beginning of July; ten days:—King ducks, 5; eider ducks, 3; long-tailed ducks, 4; sandpipers, 14; phalarope, 1; Arctic terns, 2; silver gull, 1; red-throated diver, 1. Total, 29 birds.

deep show themselves in great numbers. Seals
(*Phoca vitulina*) sport about in shoals among the
lanes of water in Wellington Channel and Barrow's
Strait; white whales and narwhals are also numerous, and the fierce-looking walrus is occasionally
seen. On a rock off Port Dundas an immense
number were discovered basking in the sun, in
August 1850. The food of these mammoths of
the ocean consists of several species of minute
Crustacea, Annelida, etc., which were dredged up
from the bottom of the sea in great quantities,
and the beautiful little *Clio borealis*, a species of
Pteropod with a transparent body and little purple
fins.

When the water appeared, we naturally felt a
strong inclination to extricate our ships from the
ice, which had held them close prisoners for more
than eleven months, and to renew the search
for our missing countrymen; accordingly a canal
was dug, that the vessels might be enabled to
approach the open water; and at the same time
charges of powder were used to blast the corner of
the ice-field which still hung on to the south-east
point of Griffith Island*. These measures were

* With 216 lbs. of powder, a space 20,000 yards in length,
and averaging 400 yards in breadth, was cleared away. The
ice varied from three to five feet in thickness, with occasional
patches of heavy grounded hummocks of ice. The estimated
weight of the ice removed, exclusive of these heavy masses, was
about 216,168 tons. The heaviest charges were of 16 lbs.,
lowered ten feet below five-feet ice.

eminently successful in their results ; and at length, on August 14th, the ice broke up, we were liberated from our winter-quarters, bade farewell to Griffith Island, anchored for a night in Assistance Bay, and on the morning of the 15th departed from the Parry Islands.

Soon afterwards the whole of the animal and vegetable life above described disappeared, and again the wide desolate ice-fields and the snow-clad hills presented themselves in all their sombre majesty and deathlike silence, unbroken now by the merry laugh and joyous mirth of Captain Austin's happy squadron.

Two lofty cairns were erected on Griffith Island and Cape Martyr, as memorials that we wintered in the adjacent floe, and the solitary grave of him who died in the execution of his sacred duty will be found by future navigators on the limestone beach. A neatly carved oaken board tells his short, sad story, and a border of moss and saxifrage is sown around his last resting-place.   On his grave the latter plant was sown in the shape of an anchor, to denote the profession to which he belonged, as well as the hope which we trust attended his dying moments,—the last touching attention of those messmates with whom he had suffered, and among whom he died.

Such are the gloomy, frozen tracts of Arctic country which compose the Parry Islands.   Scattered remains of Esquimaux encampments, hun-

I

dreds of years old, are to be found along the beach in every direction from Melville Island to Cape Warrender—vestiges doubtless of the migration of Asiatic tribes to the westward, and mournful tokens of the sterile wretchedness of these regions, so unproductive that even the Esquimaux were forced to leave them, and seek in Greenland the means of preserving a miserable existence. These ruined huts, however, are suggestive of the origin of the Greenlanders, and together with the resemblance in language, religion, and physical appearance, point out Siberia as the original cradle of the Esquimaux race.

The Shaman of Siberia is a mere conjuror, who professes to evoke the good and evil spirit, and is the counterpart of the Angekok or Magician of Greenland, who is supposed to have a *Tornguk* or familiar spirit. The language of the Asiatic nomades also strongly resembles that of the Greenlanders : they are both of the class containing monosyllabic roots, and in both the modifications of meaning are produced by the annexation of particles : they are similar also in sound. It is remarkable that both these languages are very deficient in adjectives, and there is almost a total absence of words to express abstract ideas*. Thus we find both the language and religion of the Esquimaux resemble closely those of the Siberian nomades; and when at the same time traces of their progress,

* See Baron Wrangel, ch. vi., p. 117.

from Behring's Straits to the coast of Greenland,
are to be found along the whole coast of the Parry
archipelago, North Devon, and the Carey isles;
and of the same race inhabiting the shores of
Arctic America, from Kotzebue Sound to La-
brador, there can be little doubt that they spring
from a common origin with the tribes of Northern
Asia.

The numerous remains discovered by our travelling parties conduce not a little to settle this
question, and point out the road taken by the
northern travellers. Several huts were discovered
in Melville and Byam Martin Isles. At Cape
Capel were ten ruined winter huts, with bones of
bears and seals, some of them cut with a sharp
instrument. The general form of these huts resembles an oval, with an elongated opening at one end,
and their size averages seven feet by ten: they
appear to have been roofed over with stones and
earth, and the roof is supported by the bones of
whales. All along the coast of Bathurst and Cornwallis Isles the same ruined habitations, called in
Siberia "yourts," were found, with very perfect
stone fox-traps. In Griffith Isle, too, I found five
summer huts, in one of which was part of a runner
of an Esquimaux sledge. The same deserted
yourts are scattered over Cape Warrender, Ports
Dundas and Leopold, and the Carey Islands, which
latter are within sight of the coast of Greenland.
These testimonies of the route of the emigrants

may thus be easily traced from Melville Island to the eastern shores of Baffin's Bay, where their descendants are still living.

The causes which induced this extensive migration are to be sought for in the history of northern Asia, where we find that, from the fourth to the fourteenth centuries, a powerful erratic movement was constantly prevailing. The mighty irruptions of Zengis Khan and his successors,—among others that of his grandson Sheibani, who led a horde of fifteen thousand families into the wilds of Siberia, and whose descendants reigned at Tobolskoi above three centuries, from 1242 till the Russian conquest,—were among some of the influences which drove the Siberians to migrate northward and westward; but the pressure of the warlike and restless Cossacks, and the ravages of the smallpox, were the more immediate causes.

The Jakutes, who dwell on the banks of the Kolyma, have a tradition, that they are not the first inhabitants of the country, but that many races of men had occupied the region where they now dwell. Among these were the Tunguns, the descendants of the Mongols, the conquerors of the earth, who, according to Gibbon, "insensibly degenerate into a race of deformed and diminutive savages, who tremble at the sound of arms." The Jakahirs also, the Omokis, and the Chelagis, had possession of that part of Siberia many years before various irresistible circumstances led the Jakutes to establish themselves in that country. The two latter tribes, who lived by fishing and hunting, have entirely disappeared from Siberia. The Omoki, it is said, migrated northward*.

The inhabitants at the mouths of the Lena and Kolyma formerly frequented a large island on the Polar Sea (sincè discovered by Anjou), to hunt for the bones of the fossil mammoth, and took their families with them in sledges, when it often happened that, being surprised by a thaw, they were carried away—no one knows whither—on huge pieces of ice that were rent from the larger mass; there can be little doubt that some of these hunters have been thus conveyed to the Parry Islands, and, leaving numerous traces as they went, at length reached the shores of Greenland. It is said that the fisheries of the walrus, at the mouths of the Obi, Jenesai, Lena, and Kolyma, have been known to the Chinese 2300 years, and that the large ivory tusks of that animal are greatly prized, as they retain their whiteness a long time†.

The fact therefore that numerous tribes have left Siberia,—added to their similarity in habits, shape of the features and skull, religion, language, and the vestiges of their route from Melville Island to Cape Warrender,—reduces the Asiatic origin of the Greenland Esquimaux to the closest verge of cer-

* In their passage they left numerous yourts or huts at the mouth of the Indigirka. (Wrangel, p. 181.)

† Cuvier, Ossemens Fossiles, p. 142.

tainty; and the Arctic Expedition of 1850–51, in discovering the important remains among the Parry Isles, has assisted not a little in solving this question of the peopling of Arctic America. In the Parry Islands the wretched Esquimaux was unable to exist, and famine drove him from the inhospitable coast.

CHAPTER VIII.

CONCLUSION.

A BAFFLED search is always vexatious, and when years of no ordinary privation and suffering have been voluntarily undergone in the hope of rescuing a number of our fellow-creatures from what we cannot help feeling and knowing to be a terrible fate, the disappointment and regret are increased a hundred-fold.

The season for work however had again arrived, and it was time to renew in some other direction our hitherto unavailing efforts. But whither should we go? No vestiges of the Erebus and Terror had been found beyond their winter-quarters at Beechey Island,—nothing whatever to direct our further search. To the westward, in the direction of Melville Island, they were not likely to have gone, for the whole of that coast had been carefully examined for three hundred miles, and no traces of them had been found. To the south-west of Cape Walker it was equally plain to us, from the nature of the ice, that no ships could have passed. Both sides of Wellington Channel had been examined by Mr. Penny's crews for some distance. Islands had been found to block up the passage, and here also, from the nature of the ice, it was, to say the least, highly improbable they could have passed without leaving some traces on those islands, which are said to abound in birds and eggs—those greatest of dainties to the Arctic voyager; but the sounds in the northern part of Baffin's Bay (especially Jones's Sound, where, before leaving the Orkney Islands, Sir John Franklin had expressed his intention, if other ways failed, of attempting the North-west Passage) had not yet been examined; in that direction therefore Captain Austin determined on continuing the search, previous to returning home; and accordingly the Expedition crossed the mouth of Wellington Channel, and proceeded down Barrow's Strait, which was tolerably clear of ice, on the 15th of August 1851.

Meanwhile Mr. Penny returned home, without renewing the search; and Sir John Ross, from want of provisions, also returned to England.

On arriving off Cape Warrender, Captain Austin took command of the two steamers, and proceeded to search Jones's Sound, while the Assistance and Resolute were ordered to rendezvous off Wolstenholme Sound. I landed at the foot of Cape Warrender, a lofty headland, to erect a cairn, and here

gathered a few tufts of club moss, the first speci-
mens that had been seen between this point and
Melville Island. There were also a few old deer
antlers covered with moss, and near the beach a
little Snow-bunting lay dead upon a rock.

After encountering a heavy gale of wind, and
driving for several days among the broken-up pieces
of ice in Baffin's Bay, we arrived off the Carey
Islands, a group of ten or eleven rocks, composed
of gneiss, in 76·45 north latitude. Five of them
are from one to two miles in diameter, three of
smaller size, and the remainder are nothing more
than detached rocks. The highest parts are about
four hundred feet above the level of the sea.

These islands were discovered by Baffin, who
gave them their present name; Sir John Ross
sighted them in 1818, and in 1827 a whaler must
have sent a boat on shore on one of them, as a
small cairn was found, with a piece of wood having
that date cut upon it.

Thousands of looms were breeding among the
perpendicular cliffs, and nine hundred of them
were shot by parties from the two ships; and at the
foot of the thickly inhabited rocks, large patches
of the scurvy-grass (*Cochlearia Grœnlandica*) were
growing, which we used as a salad, and found by
no means unpalatable.

Leaving the Carey Islands on the 23rd of August, we arrived at our rendezvous of Wolstenholme Sound, and there awaited with considerable

anxiety the arrival of the Pioneer and Intrepid. In the distance we had the rugged coast of Greenland, unapproachable by reason of the ice which lined the shores, while masses of loose ice surrounded the ships.

Meanwhile the steamers had coasted along the glacier-bearing shores of North Devon, and entered Jones's Sound, a broad and open strait, measuring at the entrance about sixty miles from shore to shore, and bounded by lofty granite hills rising to a height of two thousand feet, and terminating in rugged peaks. The glaciers in many places reach to the sea, and numerous icebergs were seen, apparently just detached from the parent ice-mountain.

Having proceeded up the south side of Jones's Sound for forty-five miles, the progress of the steamers was arrested by a fixed barrier of ice extending completely across, about twenty-five miles. A cairn was therefore erected on an island in the Sound, and both sides having been carefully examined, without any traces of the missing Expedition being found, the steamers passed out of this noble strait, having discovered at its entrance a large island, since called Cobourg Island; they then attempted to proceed towards Smith's Sound, but the immense chains of huge icebergs checked their progress, and at length they found themselves off the coast of Greenland and near the entrance of Whale Sound, where they were for several days in great peril of being dashed to pieces. On the 27th of August the Intrepid was driven by a field of ice against a large iceberg two hundred feet high with a terrific crash. Her destruction seemed inevitable, but the hopes of her crew were speedily revived by observing that she was gradually rising to the pressure. At 9 p.m. the pressure became intense, forcing her taffrail forty feet, and her bow thirty feet, above the level of the sea; the masses of ice running nearly ten feet above her bulwarks, and piled up one above another in a frightful manner. One whale-boat and the dingy were crushed, while the timbers of the vessels cracked and groaned, threatening all on board with destruction.

At 2 p.m. on the following day the pressure eased off, and the Intrepid was saved almost miraculously. The steamers joined the ships, the one on the 2nd and the other on the 6th of September.

The Intrepid was visited, while off the coast of Greenland, by the Arctic Highlanders, who had been seen by us in August 1850, and were supplied with clothing and other comforts. One of these people had lived on board the Assistance during the whole winter, and, though slow to learn English, had by his constant cheerfulness and good-humour, and his willingness to make himself useful, become a general favourite. He returned with us to England, and is now entered as a student at St. Augustine's College, Canterbury.

Taking into consideration the impossibility of reaching a secure harbour, the certainty if we wintered in any exposed part of Baffin's Bay of being drifted away into the Atlantic early in the spring, and the advanced season of the year, Captain Austin determined, agreeably to the spirit of his instructions, to return to England; and accordingly, after a good passage from Cape Farewell, we arrived off Scarborough in the end of September, and at Woolwich on the 1st of October, having been seventeen months absent, and sixteen without receiving any news or tidings of our friends.

Thus concluded the exertions of Captain Austin's Expedition in search of Sir John Franklin. The whole coast of the Parry Islands, from Beechey Island (where Mr. Penny had discovered the winter-quarters of the missing Expedition) to the extreme western point of Melville Island—a distance of 350 miles—had been carefully searched; besides this, vast tracts of land, extending over more than five hundred miles, had been thoroughly examined by Mr. Bradford and Lieutenant Aldrich. To the southward also of Cape Walker four hundred miles was discovered, and as far as possible surveyed and explored. Jones's Sound was then examined, and both sides of Wellington Channel had been traced by Mr. Penny to a considerable distance; yet not a vestige was to be found of the ill-fated Erebus and Terror.

Though the main object remains unattained, yet the field for future expeditions has been considerably narrowed. We now know that the Franklin Expedition did not proceed towards Melville Island or Cape Walker: it is also highly improbable that they passed up Wellington Channel, which is blocked up by islands, and in which a current runs at the rate of five miles an hour; and the northern sound of Baffin's Bay is the only outlet which has not been searched. The probability therefore of their having been destroyed in Baffin's Bay, in attempting to return home, or while enclosed by the ice, and having drifted helplessly along, as Sir James Ross did in 1849, and the American expedition in 1850–51, becomes very strong.

It would be mere trifling in one who has seen those barren, frozen regions to hold out a hope that, without provisions or ammunition, and with the cold of that rigorous climate undermining and weakening their constitutions for seven years, any of those gallant men who followed Sir John Franklin in 1845, full of enthusiasm, can still survive. Much is said about the "club-moss," which, it is affirmed, might easily be used for fuel, when there is not a single specimen from Cape Warrender to Melville Island,—and a great deal also about the abundance of animal life. So far as we saw, there is not a living thing, save a few wary bears and foxes, from September to May; and even in the summer months, without powder or shot, birds could not be obtained to support a hundred, or even fifty men for a month. We hear also of a theory about a polar basin, and a warm climate far to the northward; yet experience shows that the farther north Mr. Penny went in Wellington Channel, the colder was the climate*; and in 1827 Sir Edward Parry saw immense fields of ice drifting from the northward when in 82° north. But for those, I repeat, who have themselves felt the piercing cold, and seen the impossibility of men sustaining life on their own resources on those bleak and barren shores, it would be heartless wickedness to hold out delusive hopes to the friends and relatives of those brave but unfortunate men.

A possibility, a remote and unlikely one indeed, but still a possibility, remains; that the Erebus and Terror may have passed up Wellington Channel, far out of reach of Mr. Penny's travelling parties, and there, as Lady Franklin still sanguinely hopes, they may still be found. But not only have no vestiges of their progress been discovered, either on the shores of the channel itself or on the islands, (described as abounding in birds during the summer,) but the land also on both sides seemed to

* The heat up Wellington Channel decreases with an increase of latitude. Mr. Manson's Meteorological Journal at Assistance Bay:—Mean temperature in the shade, May the 11th to June the 8th, 1851, +19·9 Fahr. Dr. Sutherland's Journal:—Mean of ten observations from his leaving 75° north to his return to it, highest latitude attained being 76·20° north (during the same time), +16·5 Fahr.—*Blue-book*, p. 121.

close in and form a large bay, the distance between
the two extreme points seen being only marked on
the charts as twenty-five miles.

It is also just within the range of possibility that
Sir John Franklin may have penetrated up Jones's
or Smith's Sounds, and that there the remains of
his vessels are to be found; but whether any of
these remote shores still frown upon this ill-fated
Expedition, or whether, as is more probable, the two
ships have met the fate which has attended so many
whalers before and since, and been crushed to pieces
by the ice, there can be but little hope that any survivors still remain; for even if it were possible that
all the hardships and privations, the cold and hunger, of so many years in the Arctic regions could
have been withstood, it is incredible that no part
of the Expedition should have attempted to reach
either the whalers in Baffin's Bay, or the beach
where the Fury was wrecked, at which point they
knew provisions had been left; or the continent of
America, where they would in all probability have
fallen in with one or other of the numerous parties
which were last year traversing the Parry Islands
and the north of America in search of them.

But, as has been before stated, the possibility yet
remains of the vessels being still in existence; and
acting on that possibility, Government has sent
forth another expedition, that every spot of ground
in the Arctic regions, north and west of the Parry
Islands, might be thoroughly searched.   Captain

Collinson's vessels are now pressing eastward from
Behring's Straits, while other ships have been
fitted out for further search by way of Baffin's
Bay.

The same four vessels which composed Captain
Austin's expedition, with the North Star stationed
at the mouth of Wellington Channel as a depôt
in addition, left England at the end of April, 1852,
under the command of Sir Edward Belcher. Many
of Captain Austin's officers form part of the new
expedition; no longer buoyed up by the joyous
hope entertained when last they sailed—of rescuing the crews of the Erebus and Terror from their
icy prisons,—but sustained by the noble resolution
of exploring the unknown regions to the northward
of Wellington Channel and Baffin's Bay, and of
risking their lives, and suffering the well-known
hardships which such an adventure must entail, to
discover the fate of those adventurous spirits they
are in search of.

M'Clintock is amongst them, that gallant officer
so frequently mentioned in these pages, who performed the most wonderful Arctic journey ever recorded, and whose experience is surpassed by no
man living; and Osborn, who discovered so much
of Prince of Wales's Land, who commanded and
does still command the Pioneer with so much zeal
and ability; and whose zeal will enable him to entertain a last fond hope for the safety of the missing
brave, many of whom were his companions in arms

in the Chinese war. There too is Mecham, the discoverer of the extensive Island of Russel,—Hamilton, whose name is connected with the search of Young and Lowther Isles; McDougall, the explorer of that great bay which bears his name, and several others.

God speed their noble exertions! May they be more successful in this their second undertaking than they were in their first; may they again add vast tracts of land to the map of the known world; may they return to receive due praise for their noble self-sacrifice; and above all, may they at length discover the fate of Sir John Franklin's Expedition, and unravel the mystery which as yet hangs over it.

Here then we must pause, till we are in possession of further intelligence. I have endeavoured, in this short and imperfect sketch, to show how Greenland was first discovered; to point out the motives which led its several visitors and settlers to direct their steps thither; and to relate the various features of its history. How at last, in searching for a North-West Passage, the Parry archipelago was discovered by the great man whose name it bears, and how voyage after voyage followed, until at length Sir John Franklin was lost amid its tortuous mazes.

The narrative of the searching Expedition which followed has been from my own experience; and if in these pages I have been enabled to carry the minds of my readers through the stirring events

K

which occurred on the gloomy continent of Greenland, along which the Expedition of Franklin passed,
and to picture to them the wild and bleak, yet grand
and awe-inspiring, scenery of the Parry Islands,
where his last traces were discovered, and where the
efforts of our own Expedition were exerted, my
object is gained, and my humble endeavours have
succeeded in leading them to the Arctic Regions,
in Franklin's footsteps.

ZERO,

OR

HARLEQUIN LIGHT*

CHARACTERS.

THE SUN . .	} *Good Spirits.*
DAYLIGHT . .	
ZERO	
BEAR	
FROSTBITE . .	
ICEBERG . . .	*Evil Spirits in the shape*
HUNGER . . .	*of Arctic horrors.*
SCORBUTUS . .	
FOX	

Tracking and Travelling Party of Four.

DRESSES.

ZERO.—Full frosted wig, surmounted by a fanciful crown; long flowing beard; loose white robes with large sleeves, icicles hanging from different parts. Large thermometer with slide at Zero, and 50 marked on it in large letters.

FROSTBITE.—Tight dress; upper third of body and limbs white; middle red; lower blue, passing into black; long frosted wig.

HUNGER.—Long thin mask face, pale dress, loose and scanty.

SCORBUTUS.—Tight white dress, covered with purple and reddish-brown spots; mask pale, with bluish-red and blotched mouth.

GOOD SPIRIT.—Clothed in white, with chaplet and fancy wand.

* See above, p. 77.

K 2

*Scene in the Arctic Regions. One of the ships in a
perilous situation, nipped by ice; icebergs and moving
floes drifting past. Strong blue light thrown across
the stage. Drums, whistles, and all sorts of discord
by Band.* ZERO *enters, and walks majestically up
and down the stage; one or two of his Imps pass
quickly across the stage at the back.*

ZERO *advances to the front.*

ZERO. Old Christmas has almost usurp'd our rights,
Frighten'd me! *Zero!* with his roaring nights;
But ah! I'll be revenged, when on the floe
These boisterous Tars shall find it all no go.
In Melville Bay he's sought to use his might,
When lo! they blast and cut out of his sight.
And there they found a Penny * that would pass,
Made of good metal, not of spurious brass.
Their progress once or twice I did arrest,
By closing floes and hummocks† thickly press'd;
They laughed, and took to playing quoits and rounders,
Captains, officers, and seven-pounders‡;
But I am formed for action, and each word
Shortens the time and makes revenge absurd;
I'll summon Frostbite, for by education
He laughs at feelings and destroys sensation;
With papers, plays, and *soirées* they defy,
Up to this moment my supremacy;
With magic-lantern and the *bal masqué,*
They think to cheat me,—don't I wish they may!

* Mr. Penny, who commanded the mercantile expedition.
† Floes and hummocks—masses of ice.
‡ The ice quarter-masters:—old seamen who received £7 a
month. Hence the nickname.

They've turn'd a steamer* into a saloon,
And tried to *gase* me with a news balloon.

> [*Calls* FROSTBITE.

Frostbite, you idle rogue, quick, quick appear!

> *Enter* FROSTBITE.

FROST. Master, your pale and rigid slave is here.

ZERO. Wait! I am in humour for reflection,
Of which beware you freeze not in connection.
Dark Winter too his course doth quickly run,
Hasten'd by their good-fellowship and fun;
My imps of horror they have laugh'd to scorn,
Two dreaded, still remain a hope forlorn.

> [*Calls in a loud tone.*

Scorbutus, hither come, and Hunger fierce!
They well, I know, can any bosom pierce.

> *Enter* SCORBUTUS *and* HUNGER.

SCOR. and HUN. What would our gracious liege
that we should do?

ZERO. Try when within your grasp if they be true.
Begone, and loiter not! Away! be quick!
My spirits falter, I must have music;
I love operas, Bellini's or a Verdi,
Play "Sich a gettin' upstairs I never did see."

> [*Band plays the air:* ZERO *walks majestically up
> and down, keeping time with his thermometer,
> then looks out at the side-scenes.*

(*To* FROSTBITE.) Confound those imps! they move uncommon slow;
Go! call them back, more speed they ought to show.

> [*Exit* FROSTBITE.

* The Intrepid.

Enter SCORBUTUS *and* HUNGER, *about to speak.*

In haste I sent you there, my word I pledge,
And off you move as if you dragged a sledge.
Call my slaves here!
     [HUNGER *goes out and brings in Imps.*
    I think it right to mention
There's steam against us,—curse the fast invention!
          [*Singing without.*
I hear some singing on the floe.
   [*Men sing* "The sailor loves his bottle, oh!" *at
   first in a low tone, then gradually increasing
   as they pass over the stage.*
They come this way,—begone and hide awhile!
At dangers they do nothing else but smile.
          [*Exit* ZERO.
   TRACKING PARTY, *singing, pass across the stage,*
   DAYLIGHT *seen as Good Spirit hovering over
   them.*

   Enter ZERO, *following the men.*

ZERO. Oh they've passed me! Who, am I to blame?
What's Zero if his imps grow tame?
My power o'er these men is minus rather,
Yet Fahrenheit of cold has made me father.
          [ZERO *goes out.*

   DAYLIGHT *descends from above as a Good Spirit,
   and advances to the front.*

  DAYL. I dream'd, when slumber hung upon mine
    eyes.
Of love, of hope, and Arctic enterprise,
When a soft voice broke through my troubled dreams,
In tones as clear and liquid as are mountain strea ms

I rose, for well the music charm'd my watchful ear,
Turn'd and beheld a pensive maiden near.
She did entreat me in an earnest way,
But with your leave I'll sing her simple lay.   [*Sings.*

THE MAIDEN'S SONG.

AIR—"*Farewell to the Mountains.*"

Bright Spirit of light, grant thy powerful aid,
Guide England's bold sons where the missing have stray'd;
Or lend me thy swiftness, I'll rush through the air,
Their efforts encourage, their doubtful fate share.

Quite pale are the stars when morning appears,
And pale are our faces with love's silly fears;
Asleep or awake, we still mutter a prayer,
That success may soon give them again to our care.

Oh! speed thee, each moment with danger is fraught,
All bosoms are sad till good tidings are brought;
Bear with thee our sighs on thy life-cheering ray,
And chase with thy gay beams their sorrows away.

Knowing that lovers' songs ne'er have an end,
My help at once I promised her to lend;
Then hither came, I hope to find you well,
But don't expect I've any news to tell.

[*Looks out at side-scenes.*

Oh! here comes ZERO: now's the time to act;
His spirit's low—he's minus, that's a fact.
I'll hide, and counteract his evil deeds:
How fierce he'll be to find he ne'er succeeds.

[*Exit.*

Enter ZERO, *pushing down a slide on the thermometer.*

ZERO. It's time for me to make a noise and fuss,
So to begin, go down fifty minus*.
It's not a bad thermometer, I tell ye,
Better than Carey's, or a Pastorelli† ;
Besides, when Mercury begins to freeze,
It shows exactly thirty-nine degrees.

> [*Looks out at side-scenes.*

Another chance—oh! then indeed I'm blest.
Hear! all my slaves, attend to my behest.
When they have pitched their tent, your work begin,
Till then begone! and hide you all within.
They come—away, the times are out of joint,
When I am forced to tell you all avaunt.

> *Enter Sledge-party, who encamp at the back of the stage.* DAYLIGHT *seen at the side where the sledge enters.*

OFFICER. We'll pitch our tent—this seems a shelter'd place.

> [FROSTBITE *passes across behind first man.*

By Jove! you've got a frostbite on your face;
Rub, rub it well! lucky it is but slight.
(*To the other men*). Look smart there with the things
—don't be all night!

1st MAN. Tom, if those were here as plann'd these cruises,
How jolly hard they'd rub their ancient noses.

---

* That is 82° below freezing-point,—the lowest we experienced.

† There had been a dispute as to which were the best thermometers,—Carey's, Pastorelli's, or Newman's.

We've dragged all day, and now we're tired quite.
Get what we want, a stunning appetite.
    2nd MAN (*finishing the tent*).
There, that's all right—just pass the rum and can,
I'll light the stove, and cook the pemmican.
I wonder how my Peg would like these "wittles."
Scissors! I've burnt my finger with the "Kittles."
    3rd MAN (*drinking*).
I'm very thirsty, when the rum I sip
The pannikin sticks fast unto my lip.

> OFFICER *enters tent with* 3rd MAN. 2nd MAN *seen at entrance taking off his boots without his mits.* 1st MAN *near the sledge arranging its contents.* *Enter* FOX *stealthily at side.*

ZERO. Now, Frostbite, quickly! do your work right
    well,
And fix his hand fast in your icy spell.
> FROSTBITE *touches man's hand, which becomes fixed.*

2nd MAN. Confound it all, I'm bitten in the thumb.
How soon your flesh becomes cold, white, and numb.
> DAYLIGHT *waves her wand over the man's hand, and it returns to its former state.*

2nd MAN. Well, that's all right; and now to have
a smoke.
> FOX *enters, and steals a piece of pork.* 1st MAN *runs after him, exclaiming,*

Bring me the gun! Oh! here's a precious joke:
A fox has stolen a piece of this day's pork.
    3rd MAN (*from tent*).
That's what I call uncommon stupid work.

1st MAN *pushes sledge towards side, and enters tent.*

1st MAN *looks out of tent.*

What do you think of our Ventilation*?
Does it meet your learned approbation?
We have no theories when in a tent,
Nor care which way the foul air finds a vent;
We bag our heads, then smoke ourselves to sleep,
And huddling close, each other warm we keep.

                                   [*Shuts tent door.*

ZERO. Bravo, my fox! go fetch Dean's† model bear;
The morning dawns, now I for work prepare.
If I don't freeze them as they lie asleep,
May I no other promise ever keep!
Ah! now some pleasures come indeed at last:
How sound they sleep; I have them "hard and fast."

    ZERO *enters tent; his imps leave the stage;* HAR-
        LEQUIN *leaps through the Sun‡, and changes
        (the Good Spirit)* DAYLIGHT *into* COLUM-
        BINE; *they dance a pas de deux.*

    BEAR *enters and prowls round the tent;* HAR-
        LEQUIN *slaps the ground near the tent, which
        disappears, leaving the* CLOWN *grinning and
        making faces; he sees the* BEAR, *becomes
        dreadfully alarmed, and makes off for a gun;
        returns, snaps the gun, which refuses to go
        off; the* BEAR *approaches, when he succeeds
        in firing at it;* BEAR *falls, and out roll* 2nd

* There had been much dispute among the learned doctors of the squadron as to the best mode of ventilating the ships.

† Mr. Dean, the ingenious carpenter, who made a bear for the pantomime.

‡ An oiled-silk sun which rises at the back scene.

CLOWN *and* PANTALOON, HARLEQUIN *slap-
ping the ground near the* BEAR.

HARLEQUIN *and* COLUMBINE *retire;* CLOWNS
commence tumbling and fooling with PANTA-
LOON.

1st CLOWN (*to* PANTALOON). Why, what animal are
you?

PANT. A man.

1st CLOWN. How can that be, when you were got
by a bullet out of a bear? Ho! ho! ho! you fool!

PANT. Give us an account of your late proceedings.

1st CLOWN. Well, here goes.   [*Sings.*

> I'm fond of sport, that is of fun:
> I saw a bear, and took my gun;
> Away I went, at a great pace,
> My foot it slipp'd in the wrong place,
> So down I fell, when in a trice
> I popp'd through a thin young crust of ice.
> > Tol, lol, idi, idi, idi, idi, aido.

> I crusty grew: it was not fair:
> To get a wet I couldn't a bear;
> I dragged myself upon the floe,
> The bear came near; oh! what a go!
> I pulled the trigger, but the cap
> Quite finished me, by one false snap.
> > Tol, lol, etc.

> My legs they shook; my heart, pit pat,
> Hit my backbone a loud rat-tat.
> He snuffed in me a morning meal,
> And thought to fix on me his *seal;*
> When lo! I thought of boys who put
> Their head 'tween legs when bulls would butt.
> > Tol, lol, etc.

Place caps in mouth, and horrid shout,
The bulls they go to the right about;
I tried the dodge, when, bless my eyes!
The bear stood still, quite in surprise:
I gave a shout, he show'd his heels,
Oh, lor! says I, much better I feels.
Tol, lol, etc.

The moral of this round let it pass.
Bears may make tragedy of farce;
So if your fun that way doth tend,
Take my advice and take a friend:
Should you miss fire he takes your place,
Frightens the brute with his ugly face.
Tol, lol, etc.

2nd CLOWN (*to* PANTALOON). What foxes are easiest to shoot?

PANT. Sleeping foxes?

2nd CLOWN. No, not so bad either.

PANT. Running? walking? etc.

2nd CLOWN. Tame ones, to be sure.

1st CLOWN. What house in this neighbourhood is the coldest?

2nd CLOWN. Mrs. Corset's?

1st CLOWN. No.

2nd CLOWN. What then?

1st CLOWN. Why, the transit observatory, to be sure, first turning past Nelson's Monument.

2nd CLOWN. How so?

1st CLOWN. Because no one ever "heard" of its having had a warming*. Ha! Ha!

* The Observatory: a snow edifice, which, on its completion, was to have had a house-warming at the expense of Mr. Cheyne, the learned astronomer; but from some reason the promised entertainment never took place.

2nd CLOWN. Then, I'd chain up the builder.

1st CLOWN. What good would that do, stupid? Well, why would you?

2nd CLOWN. Because he ought to have known no house can stand there unless it's had a wet.

> 1st CLOWN *fetches in a fox-trap, and places it at back of stage. All run off and watch it. White fox enters, and the trap falls. Enter* CLOWNS, *who open the trap.* HARLEQUIN *slaps the trap, and out comes E. York*.*

1st CLOWN. Why, a real native! Why is he like a man with a bad cold?

2nd CLOWN. Answer it yourself.

1st CLOWN. Isn't he a little H(Uskey)†?

2nd CLOWN. Why is the Royal Arctic Theatre like Covent Garden Market?

1st CLOWN. Because it's often filled with the fresh and spicy?

2nd CLOWN. No. Because it's supported by flowers and fruit‡.

1st CLOWN. Why would you like to join the tenders?

2nd CLOWN. I should have a chance of keeping the steam up, and going ahead when I was screwed.

2nd CLOWN. It's my turn now for guessing the last. Here you are: why do all actors think the drop-scene like a tyrant?

1st CLOWN. Not being one, could not possibly say.

2nd CLOWN. Well then, because they are released and rejoiced at its fall.

* The Esquimaux we had on board.
† One of the whalers' names for an Esquimaux.
‡ The decorations of the front.

*Enter people coming from a masquerade, walk about the
stage,* CLOWNS *joking them.*

Sedan chair enters with a masked female in costume.
CLOWNS *run and bonnet chairmen, and open the door,
drag out the female, one lugging one way, the other
the opposite.* HARLEQUIN *enters; they put her back
into the chair, and commence to fight.* HARLEQUIN
passes quickly; slaps the back of the chair.

1st CLOWN, *having knocked down* 2nd CLOWN, *goes to
the chair, opens the door, when out steps North
Polar Star in rough dress, treads on* CLOWN'S *toe,
advances to the front, and sings.*

AIR—*Ivy Green.*

A noble soul has that man, I ween,
  Who braveth these regions cold:
No dangers that threaten his life are seen
  When he seeketh the brave and bold.
Oh! the heart must be hard and bad indeed,
  Or ruled by a coward's whim,
If it bounds not to think of the friendly deed
  Perform'd in these lands by him.
    Seeking where the lost have been,
    A gallant band may yet be seen.

Through ages long past, the British name
  Has been known in every clime,
And all must trust that the well-earn'd fame
  Will endure to the end of time.
To rescue from death the friend, or foe,
  Was ever the sailor's boast;
And now, 'mid the terrors of frost and snow,
  His courage is needed most.
    Seeking, etc.

Soon night will be past, and spring draweth nigh,
  To gladden us all again,
When we'll seek around, with a watchful eye,
  Nor at any toil complain.
They await us in England, the beauteous, the fair,
  When our dangerous task is o'er,
And who would not greater hardships dare
  To be prized by them once more?
    Seeking, etc., etc.

[*Exeunt* OMNES. *Enter* HARLEQUIN *and*
COLUMBINE, *who dance a pas de deux.*
CLOWNS *and* PANTALOON *enter, followed by men bringing in balloon gear. The* CLOWNS *drive off the men,
and inflate balloon, which, when full, takes up* 1st
CLOWN, *who exclaims, Oh! aint I Green! After a
short time he descends without balloon, and advancing
to the front with a slip of paper in his hands, reads
news from home. All well! And a happy new year
to you! Now for my advice:*

A fool may sometimes wisdom speak,
  Though wanting youth and beauty;
    So let me say,
    In Nelson's way,
England expects that every man
This spring will do his duty.

FINALE—GRAND TABLEAU.

THE EPILOGUE

AT THE CLOSE OF THE SEASON, AT

The Royal Arctic Theatre,

28TH FEBRUARY, 1851.

When first this curtain rose, we strove to say,
All our success in your applause would lay:
Thus trusting, we have tried, and not in vain,
To hear your laughter o'er and o'er again.
One sole regret we had, until tonight,
That those so near* could not with us unite;
And in this mimic world the hours beguile,
Where all do feel the want of woman's smile.
But now 'tis o'er, the flower of day expands,
And greedy time new sacrifice demands†.
The strength of youth, the wisdom of the sage,
Must soon appear upon life's boundless stage;
Amusement then to duty will give place,
And lines of thought will mark the anxious face.
In merriment and fun we've joined together,
Defying cold and every change of weather:
Nobly each and all their means have used,
First the amusers, then in turn the amused.
In health and happiness the time has fled;
And bright success on all its rays has shed.
That our next efforts may as well succeed,
Is the great wish in which we're all agreed.

* Penny's crews and Sir J. Ross's in Assistance Bay.
† The travelling parties.

For EU product safety concerns, contact us at Calle de José Abascal, 56–1°,
28003 Madrid, Spain or eugpsr@cambridge.org.

www.ingramcontent.com/pod-product-compliance
Ingram Content Group UK Ltd.
Pitfield, Milton Keynes, MK11 3LW, UK
UKHW012340130625
459647UK00009B/423